Divi[CHARGE AGAINST EVIL

Disclaimer

In my *Divine Miracle Series*, I have recreated events, places and conversations from my recollections of them. Since many of the chapters in the first two books in this series, *Charge Against Evil* and *Hands of God* are mostly about my previous life, I have used my memories and imagination to create my characters along with their names in order to fully express the flavor and experience of that life as best I could.

In the present life chapters, I have changed some of the characters names and embellished on some dialogue for literary effect. Since I am a stickler for dates, times and places most of those are as accurate as possible.

To Frances,

I hope you enjoy
the story of my two lives

Kerry Van Dyke

2021

Divine Miracles
CHARGE
AGAINST EVIL

Memoir of a Previous and Present Life

Book One

Kerry Van Dyke

ISBN – 978-1-7361322-0-3
ISBN – 978-1-7361322-1-0 (eBook)

Edited by Michelene Landseadel
Cover design and illustrations by Kerry Van Dyke

Dedicated to and in memory of my wonderful parents,
Tom and Yvonne Van Dyke
My father taught me integrity and attention to detail
My mother taught me passion and love for the arts
And to both of my daughters, Carissa and Lara who grace me with their
love and support

CONTENTS

Introduction

When we shine our own divine light into the darkness, evil ceases to exist

Each of us has a story to tell. Where we were born, where we went to school, our first fight, our best friend, and our first long kiss. Our stories matter. My own story is no different. I'm attached to my memories like my own breath: undercurrent to my actions and life sustaining. Moreover, my experiences probably hold greater fascination to me than they do anyone else.

A few of the events I am about to unfold may come close, perhaps in circumstance, to your own experiences and for others they may be as dissimilar as midnight is to morning. Nevertheless, lessons learned, and ones not yet learned, wisdom gained, insight clouded, sorrow, compassion and confusion reveal threads common in all of our embroidered memories.

When grief and horrendous visions from a previous life suddenly rose up from my subconscious, my heart felt severed to its core. Yet after I faced most of its details and pondered writing a story about what I recalled, I initially hesitated.

Twelve years later (the moment I finally put pen to paper) the story wrote me… forging who I would become. My desire to uncover the whole truth, no matter how terrifying, turned into an obsession for healing. Writing became my only form of exorcism.

I did not know when I began this endeavor that my decision to face the evils within my previous life would bring the opposite to me—divine miracles and gifts. With newfound gifts of clairvoyance, along with a plethora of synchronicity, not only was I able to face more atrocities, I began to help others in need of clarification and resolution about previously unanswered (or unanswerable) questions in their own lives. Through this journey I discovered that having the courage to bring light into the darkness in order to see the truth is the seed of Hope Eternal.

Charge Against Evil is the first in the *Divine Miracles* series and details most of my previous life. Within *Charge Against Evil* are three chapters from my present life, which include how I recalled that life, a journey to the town and institution where my previous life took place and how facing the horrors in that life brought unexpected gifts to this current one. It is my hope that my personal journey into the 'bowels of the beast' will advance truth and light a path to freedom from the experiential chains that bind us.

Warning: I strongly suggest that when reading the sections detailing my previous life you skip any parts that are too disturbing or graphic, or, that you, at least, set them aside for a bit as some chapters are very explicit and horrific.

The Severing

Friday, January 20, 1939
Today I am thirty-eight. Fifty-one years ago, I was twelve.

With my eyes shut, I smell damp buffalo skin draping the frame of my teepee. The rain tapping on the taut hide sounds like drumming in the distance. Colorful feathered headdresses bow back and forth to the resonant beat, and the low hum of men in their dance....

With my eyes shut, I see crimson bougainvillea framing the uncovered window, clouds of dawn cracking open, sending bright orange beams onto the wide glistening sea below my Moroccan villa. Slowly, I breathe in moist, salty air....

With my eyes shut, I am in the city teeming with morning traffic, horns honking, mothers yelling for their sons to watch out, children running and laughing on their way to school. Now, I can no longer keep my eyes shut.

Now, with eyes wide open, I see black-barred windows set high in the wall of my tiny room. The sun vanishes behind a thick sheet of gray and rain slaps hard on dingy panes. I used to like the smell of rain, but not here. Here, the air harbors odors of unwashed, bed-ridden bodies that the rain, no matter how hard it showers, cannot wash away.

Of all the places in this vast world, of all the places to wake up to, why do I wake up in this locked room, awaiting sounds of shuffling feet in the hall, demanding voices and the morning bell? I want to close my eyes once more where the vision set before me would be my new reality. I want to be like the sun and vanish behind a thick cloud, and people would just wonder, "Where has she gone?"

A loud, determined sound, "Pound, pound, pound!" slammed at my door, startling me. A moment later, it opened.

I pulled the rough brown blanket up over my head. Not today, please not today.

"Get up Sarah," shouted a gruff voice. "The doctor wants to see you now!"

I knew exactly who it was. Without even looking, I pictured him standing there waiting for me to get out of bed. He was just plain ugly.

He had large hairy arms that always propped away from his fat body. My name for him was 'Ape-man' but apes seemed much more respectable. His cheeks sagged. His large lips were always open, and wet, as if he was getting ready to eat an ice cream on a hot day. Maybe if I didn't move a muscle, he'd think me dead and go away.

But I remember everything.

Hans jerked my blanket back, sending it to the floor. Instinctively, I pulled my knees up under my gown and held them tightly to my chest.

"Get up!" he demanded with his bristly German accent.

I scooted up slowly, trying to keep my legs secure, and slid my back against the cold wall.

He grabbed my ankles, "There will be no time for that now," and yanked on them hard to straighten out my legs in front of me. "Dr. Cox will be here in a few minutes to see you."

Slowly, he bent down close to me, almost in my face. I stopped breathing, attempting to avoid the putrid smell from his unwashed teeth. The corners of his mouth turned up slyly and his groping hand came at me. I crossed my arms over my chest and decided that if his hand got any closer, I would bite it hard. The door opened. Hans quickly pulled away—acted completely innocent—and ran to hold the door open for Dr. Cox.

I don't want to see him. I don't want to be here. I want to go home. Please, I just want to go home!

Dr. Cox turned to Ape-man, casually directing him, "Go get the cart I prepared. It's at the nurses' station."

The doctor did not pay attention to me, not yet anyway. He stood near the door, flipping through papers on his clipboard, hardly moving.

It's peculiar how Dr. Cox—who stands much shorter than Hans, seems bigger and even more frightening. I do not like him at all, even when he tries to sound nice. He's ugly too, but in a different way than Hans. Out walks Ape-man and in slithers Snake-man. Then, the word impenetrable pops into my head. Yes, he is that.

Dr. Cox began scratching down words on the clipboard, glancing at his watch, and making loud taps with his pen, like placing a period at the end of a very important sentence. His face sprouted gray stubbles, appearing rough and wrinkly. He wore a white cap tightly on his head and the strings lay loose and untied in the back, as if he put it on in a hurry, was ready to take it off, or just didn't care. Impenetrable.

I was staring at his cap when his head tilted up ever so slightly. The two tiny black dots suggesting eyes surrounded by steel gray looked right into me; as if he knew all along my staring at him, and creepy, as if I took pleasure in what I saw. I didn't like him at all.

He peered at me and spoke slowly and oddly like a forked tongue slipping from his mouth, "How are we today?"

Chills ran down my spine. This time I'm not going to answer his questions.

"Still having those nightmares?"

No matter my wish, the nightly images and panic flooded in. A steep, dark stairwell, falling and falling. Red is everywhere. I quickly answered with a cracked voice, "No-o-o."

"Are you sure?" he asked, more deliberate than before.

My eyes shut hard trying to get away from it all but evil touches me. It almost catches me as I try to run away. My body is too heavy. I can't. I can't.

His deep voice startled me, "I know you see it Sarah."

Oh, God, I didn't want to tell him again no matter what. My eyes shut tight even though that dream replayed like a movie in my head, repeatedly.

"Why don't you want to tell me? Why are you afraid?"

It's an evil monster! I know it. It's behind me, licking my neck. Why is it licking my neck? Why doesn't it go away? No!

"It's you, Sarah. You can tell me. Why did you do it?"

"No. No, it's a monster!" I turned my head to the wall and began sobbing. Even though he stopped asking me questions his presence remained palpable.

My eyes remain shut for several minutes while attempting to control grief. All I hear is the scratching of his fountain pen and his loud breathing.

Then the door opened abruptly with a thud. I wiped my eyes and saw Nurse Blanchard enter. Her repugnant face makes me wonder why everyone here looks ugly.

Nurse Blanchard is tall, unlike Dr. Cox. Each time her stern face with tight lips reminds me of something, but what? She glanced over at Dr. Cox a moment, and then motioned impatiently with her long fingers opening and closing rapidly for me to come with her.

I didn't move.

"Sarah!" she ordered loudly, "Let's go and relieve ourselves."

Dr. Cox nodded.

As my feet touched the cold floor, Hans barged back in, almost rolling over my toes with a silver cart. He stopped and positioned the cart next to Dr. Cox. As I stared at the cart, trying to figure out what it was, Nurse Blanchard grabbed me by pulling my arm, and hurried my small footsteps down the long wide hallway to the bathroom.

There was no privacy in this large square room at the end of the hall. It was damp and cold, with white tiles blanketing the floor and four walls. All that stood before me were the open toilets, Nurse Blanchard, and the squawking echo of her voice. I don't like being here.

"Hurry up, Sarah. I'm not going to stand here all day."

I tried to imagine my Moroccan home by the sea, my teepee in a field blanketed with wildflowers or being back at home, anything but being here. I wanted her to go away and I didn't want to go back to where Dr. Cox coiled.

I glanced up, hoping she would be kind enough to turn away. She didn't. She just stood there with a blank face, dressed in stark white. Her hat and uniform were so stiff with starch that when she took them off, they could stand on their own in a corner. Her arms stationed squarely on her hips rather reminded me of a photo of an army tank on a magazine cover but then it suddenly came to me; she reminds me of the vulture at the San Francisco zoo.

I couldn't urinate with her hovering above me. We exited the relieving room and went back down the hall. I became more anxious the closer we got to my room and closed my eyes to pray. Please God, don't let anything happen to me today. My fingernails flicked nervously making clicking sounds.

Vulture woman peered down at me with her eyes squinting. "Stop that."

We passed other women patients who, like caged animals in this zoo, gawked in terror while a few stared pitifully, as if knowing and sympathizing with my fate and others paid no attention at all. Why doesn't anyone notice her and her long skinny fingers with long painted nails wrapped around my forearm? Don't they see them as talons as too?

When we entered my room, she escorted me to my cot and ordered me to sit on the edge. Dr. Cox and Ape-man stood by. He nonchalantly turned to Hans and queried, "All set?"

"Yes." Hans handed a syringe to Dr. Cox.

The needle was long, and I pleaded, "I don't really want anything today. I'll be good."

"You have to be cooperative, Sarah. Now then, give me your arm," Dr. Cox said sternly.

My arm was behind my back. Hans quickly grabbed it and with a vice-like squeeze held it still. I wanted to yank it away but flashed back to a few weeks ago when I woke up in a different room crying. It was dark, and I didn't know where I was. A nurse with red hair, not mean like Vulture woman, came in to bring me warm soup. She told me I put up a big fight with the doctors when I first arrived here, which was why I ended up in the dark room. She also told me it had been four days. Four days I didn't remember. However, my body ached, and I had bruises on both of my arms and face.

"Ouch," I cried, when he jabbed in the needle. My head felt light and I lay back on my cot, quietly slipping away, distanced from what was happening around me, floating in and out of a dream.

Two orderlies transferred my now limp body onto a gurney and wheeled me out of the room. I wanted to keep my eyes open to see where we were going, but it was so hard. We rolled down the long hallway past other rooms, past other patients, until we came to some double doors. Beyond the doors was a dimly lit square hall. They wheeled me around a corner and pushed through another set of doors. It was bright. My head fell to one side. We were in a long passageway with small pane windowed walls. Through them was green; green grass glistening wet.

Slowly down the passageway we rolled, creating rhythmic sounds of wheels echoing, "Click-clunk, click-clunk, click-clunk," on the tiled floor. I wanted to keep open my eyes, but a sweet dream surrounded me.

Grandmother's face appeared. She's leaning on her cane at the bottom of the stairs staring straight up at me and I smile.

Click-clunk!" bumped the wheels jolting me abruptly out of the vision. Again, through the slits of my heavy lids, there is green and glints of rain on the many panes and a gray-masked sky. I wanted to be alert, but my eyes fell shut. Each time they closed the slow, metronomic sounds transported me to the same vision beckoning me. Each time they closed, I traveled further and further away, down a different hall, until I stepped through a window in time.

"Sarah, Sarah," calls Grandmother. "Sarah? Can you hear me?"

"Yes, Grandmother, I'm coming," I shout, bounding down the stairs.

At the bottom stands Grandmother, chiding me with her polished cane. "It's about time, you know."

"Yes, Grandmother," I interrupt. "When dinner is served, I should not have to be yelled for."

"Precisely. How many times must I tell you this?"

"Oh, about five hundred, I imagine."

"Well then," she begins, acting as if she were counting on her fingertips, "according to my figures, I will only have to remind you two more times and you will remember it for the rest of your life."

"Oh, Grandmother."

I help her into her chair at one end of the dining room table and sit beside her. While folding the napkin properly on my lap, I glance at Grandmother and notice a faint smile forming on her pursed lips.

Our dinners are always formal. Nan prepares all our meals and eats with us—except when we are having guests. If we are, between serving us each course, she eats in the kitchen. Even though Nan is like a second mother to me, and the house can't run smoothly without her, Grandmother insists upon this formality.

We drink wine—mine has water in it—bottled from our own vineyards. Grandmother always blesses our meal and proposes a different toast to begin each one, unless a friend is ill. Then we would wish them well each day of their sickness. Each toast is short, wise and to the point.

Poised, both Nan and I await Grandmother's cue. Her thoughtful face and white hair glimmer in the soft light of the candles. She wears her favorite freshly pressed navy-blue linen dress with white piping. She is ready; she looks at Nan, then smiles at me.

"May the future be now," she says, lifting her glass to meet our glasses simultaneously. "Clink. Clink."

A calloused thumb lifted one of my eyelids suddenly interrupting me from the memory of that bitter yet pleasing flavor under my tongue. Why is this man staring at me so? He walked away and disappeared into a room across the hall. Just before the door shut, he spoke.

"Dr. Cox. She's not awake yet."

The long hallway has two doors at the end. I thought that I was outside of my own bedroom at home but realized I was in the hospital in a different hall and not at home. How long have I been asleep? What happened?

A lumbering shape pushed open the dark red door and came out of the room across the hall. It was a man. He seemed familiar. Oh my God, it's Ape-man! Quickly, my eyes shut, fearing the worst and hoping he would ignore me and go away, but my gurney began to move. As it rolled down the hall I remembered. Dr. Cox wanted to do something. But why here? What was going to happen to me, or did something happen already, and I can't remember?

Through a slit in my eye I saw we were heading for the red door. Many voices inside were speaking all at once blurring into an indistinct din. The moment he wheeled me in all became silent and I quickly shut my eyes. Yes, I knew that the many voices had many eyes and they were now all upon me. I remain motionless.

Ice-cold fingers touched my head and slipped something snug around it. Then the cold hands bound my wrists and feet. I wanted to shake my head out of the fog but didn't dare. Then, I decided they mustn't know I hear them. I tried my best to wake up fully and tried not feeling numb from that stupid injection, but sleep beckoned me.

My heavy lids opened slowly. Have I been asleep for hours? When I saw so many people all around me talking, I realized where I was, closed my eyes and remained still.

The voices, once stifled by my presence, were alive in conversation. Inconspicuously, my eyes opened to a slit and I was able to slowly peer around the room. There were several men standing about talking. No one seemed to be watching or notice that I was awake. I could hear Dr. Cox just to my left and another voice that sounded familiar. My head throbbed as I turned ever so slightly to see who it was.

He wore a brown suit and held a black hat that turned slowly in his hands. I felt like I should know him but didn't. Another man in a white coat turned and started walking towards me. I softly closed my eyes. A calloused thumb lifted my eyelid while I pretended to be asleep.

"Not quite ready," said the man.

My thoughts reeled in confusion. Ready? Why am I not ready and for what? Should I say something? Should I tell these men I shouldn't be here? Fear spread through me, yet I couldn't run. I couldn't show my hatred or anger for I knew that would be a worse fate. All I could do was pretend to be asleep.

Time stopped. My soul begged to scream, to turn to someone for help. I couldn't show anger or hatred because I knew they would hurt me if I did. There was nothing I could do except wait and listen.

"Dr. Brown," asked Dr. Cox impatiently, "would you check her again? We're all set to go."

Again, the callused thumb pressed open my right eye. There was a face of a doctor I had never seen before. He seemed too young to be wearing a doctor's smock however unlike Dr. Cox, he had a kind face that assured comfort. I didn't want him to notice I was awake and as soon as he released his thumb, I closed my eye.

"Sarah," he said softly, "Sarah, are you awake?"

I kept my eyes closed and my body still.

"Dr. Cox," he began, "she's not ready just yet."

"That's strange. Are you sure?"

"Yes," said Dr. Brown.

"Well, I'll speak to our guests in just a minute then."

I heard shuffling of papers and slowly opened one of my eyes to a very tiny slit. At the other end of the small room was a group of men in dark suits. One wore a big mustache and had a camera slung around his neck. In his hand rested a silver dish. There was a bulb in it. Two other men busily scribbled on note pads. One had bushy sideburns, a big mustache and a large round belly. His hat, tilted back on his head, had a card stuck in the brim. Maybe he's a reporter and the other man his photographer? Dr. Cox was to my left, flipping through some papers on his clipboard. A few doctors and nurses were behind him.

Just to his right was that man in the brown suit, still turning his hat in his hands. He had a slender build; jet-black hair and his white face had a sad or concerned expression. I felt like I should know him. He didn't have a notepad; he didn't appear to be any kind of doctor and he had an air of sincerity that didn't match an uneasiness I sensed.

Through the slit in my eyes I watched Nurse Blanchard come to me with a white towel in her hands. She rolled it up and placed it under the small of my back. She yanked the thick brown leather straps on my wrists and ankles even tighter. They hurt. Dr. Cox turned to the group of men and began to talk.

"For over a year, this child was suffering from depression. However, the violent death of her Grandmother, who raised her, by-the-way, sent her into a much deeper emotional state."

What? My Grandmother is not dead! He must be talking about someone else. The more he spoke, the more confused I became. It seemed as if he was speaking of me, but I was sure it must be someone else. I know that she was not dead! What did they do to her?

The reporter interrupted Dr. Cox, "Why, Doctor, would this death cause such trauma, I mean, people die every day?"

"Well, Sarah's emotional problems prior to the accident were severe enough that she was on leave from her schooling for some time. When someone found her Grandmother's broken body at the bottom of their stairwell alongside her overturned wheelchair, Sarah was next to her in the corner, in a fetal position and couldn't speak."

My head pounded. My stomach churned. He's lying. I just know it. It can't be true!

"Dr. Cox," blurted out the reporter. "Why would the Grandmother attempt to come down the stairs in a wheelchair?" Before Dr. Cox could answer, he fired more questions, "Or, was Sarah violent? Do you think she was somehow responsible for her Grandmother's fall?"

The brown-suited man quickly interrupted, "Dr. Cox, I don't think it necessary to...."

"Yes, yes," responded Dr. Cox quickly, "I'll go on. I cannot go into anymore of the circumstances surrounding this patient, as you well know, but I can tell you what conditions necessitate this type of treatment."

I was certain that Dr. Cox was making all this up. They didn't know what they were saying. I wanted to scream, to spit in their faces, to run away faster than they could ever catch me, but they strapped me down like a wild beast. I knew that no one would believe me, and that if I tried to get away, Dr. Cox or Hans would certainly punish me later when the men in suits were not around. I remained frozen in fear, listening.

"Would you classify her as a paranoid schizophrenic," asked one of the men with a notepad, "the type we often hear about?"

"Well," began the doctor, "being catatonic is a syndrome of schizophrenia. The patient will go in and out of that state. However, even a person with schizophrenia can seem perfectly normal."

"You mean to say," the reporter blurted out and then glanced around the room, "that any of us could be nuts?"

"Yes, it's true that a person with paranoia can have a personality that appears normal. Let me ask you," Dr. Cox eyed the reporter's name tag, "Mr. Blake, have you ever been afraid of heights or closed-in places?"

"Oh, I get it, like when you get the willies and there's nothin' there?" affirmed Mr. Blake.

"For some it's just the willies, as you say but for others it can preoccupy their mind constantly until it begins to dominate all their activities. The difference is that with someone like Sarah, her paranoia has altered her personality. Her emotions have detached from her thought processes causing disorientation. When she first arrived, she was violent and aggressive, thinking that everyone was out to hurt her, which is a form of paranoia. She truly believes that we are a threat to her."

"But why this type of treatment?" asked Mr. Blake. "It doesn't appear to me that she would feel very safe right here, right now. I know I wouldn't!" He laughed nervously, glancing around the room, seeking the agreement of others, but no one else joined in.

"This is exactly why you are here today, Mr. Blake," began Dr. Cox. "I wanted other noted doctors and a reporter like yourself to see what state this patient is in prior to this therapy and to see for yourself how it is very successful for this type of disorder. I want the public to understand that our hospitals are not Bedlam, that they are places where there is hope for a cure."

"But why so drastic a measure?"

"Yes, exactly Mr. Blake, a drastic measure for a drastic condition. Would you like to see this beautiful young girl able to function normally again?" Dr. Cox asked Mr. Blake, who just nodded. "Well, this is our hope too."

"But she appears calm and harmless," commented Mr. Blake.

"Let me reiterate that she has been violent, severely depressed and unresponsive to any other treatment," explained Dr. Cox, exasperated. "She was sedated after all, but its effects are temporary. Now then, let us continue before…."

"Can't you just talk to her and find out what's bothering the poor child?" he interrupted.

All the eyes in the room glared at the reporter as if he would be the next.

"I'm sorry, Doctor. Silly question… please, go on."

"Thank you. I shall. This patient will receive a treatment just about every other day, depending on her recovery, for six weeks. After that we will begin psychotherapy."

I was confused and tried to comprehend what he was saying when I heard a soft voice behind me.

"Sarah?"

Before I knew, I turned, opened my eyes and found myself staring at Dr. Brown. He smiled. It was such a big, warm smile that I couldn't help but smile back.

Dr. Brown's large hand rested gently upon my forehead and he spoke, "Don't worry, little one. You'll feel better soon enough."

I wanted to say, I'm fine, I'm fine, but uselessness caged my words.

He turned to Dr. Cox and said, "Okay, she's ready, Doctor."

"All right then," Dr. Cox began, as he turned to the others in the room, "we will now commence."

Hesitantly this time, Mr. Blake spoke up, "Um, can you tell me how much electricity is going into her?"

Electricity… What does he mean? What are they going to do to me? Are they going to kill me? Did I do something bad?

"It is fed at 120 volts and only 900 milliamperes from this portable machine right here. She won't feel a thing and she won't remember anything about it. In fact, it should completely bring her out of the state she's been in, slowly after some time, of course. And, Mr. Blake, I do hope you will come back and see for yourself."

"I will. Believe me. I will."

"It will stop automatically at four-tenths of a second." Dr. Cox smiled and patted his hand on a black box with dials and gauges and wires coming out of it and said, "This is the most effective tool at this time for aiding in her recovery."

As Dr. Cox continued to talk, I was too frightened to listen anymore. My mind went in and out of a blank state. Can't someone stop this? Can't the reporter or maybe the doctor with the kind face see how horrible they are treating me? Maybe he…where is he?

Suddenly, the nurse stuffed something hard and black in my mouth. I wanted to cry, no, no! But I couldn't and looked all around the room with my eyes shrieking in terror.

"Now!" shouted Dr. Cox.

"Ah a h a h a h a h a h a h a h!"

Screeching, screeching, pain of thunder raging through the heart of mine.

Cinched my body, screaming torrents, thrashing moments out of time.

Beyond the pain, beyond all hope I slip into the abyss.

My soul cries out, I snap and jerk destroying what was this.

I cry not for what was once whole can be no more.

My soul's misplaced, they stole my heart, and death itself is borne.

Stillness

  Sudden breath   sudden breath

  Deep breath

  S p a c e   floating away

  Floating away

Darkness

The Last Dance

Distant sounds brought me slowly out of a deep sleep. I struggled to remain in my dream that I didn't want to leave. I didn't want to wake up, but my dream but my dream simply vanished. When I opened my eyes, nothing was familiar. There was a window with bars on it and beyond were tops of some dark green trees.

Where am I?

However, for some reason the answer didn't matter. I lay on a small cot, not sure of where I was. My mind lay empty and dazed beside me.

Slowly, my chest rose up, and I watched it; up, taking in stale air, then out again, up, breathing in—down, breathing out—up, breathing in—down, breathing out—up, breathing in—down, breathing out.

In my dim state of mind, no thoughts that drifted in could take root. Ideas came and left, like a silky tuft of a dandelion finding no fertile soil, slowly floating by, venturing on the wind.

After some time, I noticed that my neck ached, and a funny sensation wrapped around my forehead—tingling jitters. I tried to touch my head with my hand, but it wouldn't respond. I realized my arm was asleep and seemed to belong to another body. Finally, I was able to wiggle my fingers then raise my heavy arm to touch my brow.

I was so tired that my arm slipped down to the bed.

I turned my attention to the sheet of gray out my windows. In stillness, I watched as the clouds darkened and began to leave drops of water on the panes.

The drops seemed to speak to me as they slid down and collected on the glass, "Nothing to do, nowhere to go, nothing to be."

Footsteps sounded and stopped outside my door. I wondered, for a moment if someone was there, but hadn't the strength of body or mind to turn and see. Some time passed, and I heard footsteps sound again. This time a man entered.

He came to my side, picked up my wrist with one hand and stared at his watch. I gazed at his face all the while, when an impression drifted to my senses. His face was soft and kind, framed by deep chestnut hair combed back perfectly in place.

"How are we today?" he asked, then gently lowered my wrist to my side, placing his palm on my forehead. I felt there was something familiar about him.

"I met you yesterday, Sarah. My name is Dr. Brown." He paused and studied my face. "You look as though you are trying to place me. That's good."

Yesterday? Yesterday?? Tension filled my eyes as I tried but couldn't remember.

He patted my hand and said in a sweet voice, "Just relax. All you need to do is rest and eat. Soon, you will get your strength back."

His words simply floated above me. I lay there just breathing in and breathing out, when suddenly my whole body gave a quick jerk.

"Now don't let that little quiver upset you, Sarah. It's perfectly normal after a treatment." His rough hand gently stroked my brow.

His touch seems familiar, but why?

"I think you should try to walk around the room, and then you need to eat something." He put his hands under my arms, lifted and turned my limp body to a sitting position on the side of the cot. "Now, try and sit up."

Coldness startled my feet, and I glanced down.

"That's right, Sarah. You can walk." He pulled me up firmly and said, "Just take a few steps now. You can do it."

Suddenly, the room was spinning, and life slipped from my limbs. Dr. Brown tried to hold me up but lost his balance and fell backwards with me landing on top of him.

A moment later, I found myself gazing directly into his light blue eyes. The look on Dr. Brown's face, with raised eyebrows, eyes and mouth opened wide, made me let out a laugh. He was so pleased he hugged me right at that moment.

"See," he said. "You're going to be just fine. You just need a better dance instructor." Suddenly, the door crashed open. I turned and saw a silver cart loom directly above me.

"Don't ram into us!" yelled Dr. Brown.

A voice sounded behind the cart, "What?" Staring down was a nurse with a mean, piercing glare. Once Dr. Brown was standing, he leaned over and helped me up to sit on the edge of my bed. He did not offer any explanation as to why we were on the floor. He simply brushed himself off, wrote something down on his clipboard and said to her sternly, "Be certain she eats well, Nurse Blanchard."

Nurse Blanchard, Nurse Blanchard, that name, her face...seems like I should know her.

"Yes, Doctor," she complied.

Dr. Brown turned to me, smiled briefly and walked out the door. I felt dizzy again and lay back down. She walked to my side and retrieved a tray of food from the cart.

"Now sit up and eat!"

I tried to get up but couldn't. She came over and pulled me up.

"Now eat!" she repeated.

I don't want food! I'm not hungry! My stomach hurts. My head hurts. I don't like Nurse Blanchard!

A rush of energy rose within me. An unbridled hatred flooded my eyes, and then my body jerked violently, knocking over the table and tray.

"What in the hell are you doing?" She looked me square in the eyes and slapped my face hard.

I couldn't cry. I wanted to but couldn't. She slapped me again and I fell backwards on my cot, hitting my head on the wall.

"I told you before that you had better mind me," she said, shaking her finger. "You want me to tell Dr. Cox about this incident? I bet you can remember what he likes to do to little girls that misbehave, can't you?" she added smirking.

I found my legs, pulling them close to my chest, and began to cry as if someone else had turned on the faucet to my tears, and wasn't going to turn it off—ever.

"No food for you tonight Sarah, no matter what Dr. Brown says," she said, picking up the tray. "Don't you ever—I mean ever —do that again." She lunged, grabbed my right wrist and tied it to the straps attached to the rail on the cot. Then she grabbed my left one, tying it to the other side. "That will teach you to act up. Think about it," she squawked, as she put her face a few inches from mine and pursed her lips.

Nurse Blanchard crashed out of the room just as she had crashed in. I couldn't stop crying and wanted to hide in the comfort of my arms but wasn't able. I rolled to my side as much as the straps would allow and curled up my knees to my chest. A few minutes later, an orderly came in and cleaned the floor. Just before he left, he patted me softly on the head.

In the breath of my sorrow, I heard distant cries echoing down the hall, splattering rain on my window and Vulture-Woman orchestrating the cacophony of tears.

I turned away. All I could do was cry.

I wish everyone would leave me alone.

Patty

For this is not right these feelings I share, the feelings that bring death to the air

"Ring..., ring..., ring," sounded the loud, constant chime of the morning bell. I tried rubbing the puffiness from my eyes, but the brown straps still bound my hands to the rail. I heard rattling sounds at my door and turned to see it open and a young nurse walked in.

"Are you going to be good today Miss Sarah?" she asked me in a little voice that matched her size. It didn't seem she really expected me to answer, although her left eyebrow rose to a curious height. "My name is Nurse Crenshaw," she told me in a high-pitched southern drawl, and then turned away to face the door.

I watched her curiously. She seemed to be preparing something from a cart just outside the door.

She seems nice enough. Maybe, if I am quiet, she'll untie me.

"Nurse Blanchard said you were a bad li'l girl last night and you needed a lesson. I hope y'all learned it. You know you must do as yah told," she said peevishly.

With her back still before me, I stuck my tongue right out at her quickly, not wanting her to notice me. She turned, unaware of my salute, and walked to my bedside with pills and water in hand.

"I'll unfasten yah, but if yah cause me any problems, I will not hesitate to bring yah back and restrain y'all again!"

I nodded. After she untied my straps, I rubbed my wrists and then rolled my fingers over my eyes. My neck still hurt and when I touched it, I felt a bump on the back of my head. I sat up slowly, lightheaded.

"Ahm gonna get another patient to escort yah to the bathroom and then the cafeteria. Now y'all do as she says and don't cause her any trouble, yah hear?"

I nodded again, took the pills and she walked out the door.

I looked at the dim light through the window and noticed for the first time that I might be able to see the sun today. Even though there were some gray clouds, they were far off. Patches of bright blue sky greeted my puffy eyes and the morning sun was beginning to glisten on top of a tall, damp fir tree in the distance.

"Tap, tap, tap."

I turned my head towards the soft rapping sound. The door opened slightly. Peering in to greet me was a young girl. She smiled as she shyly walked towards me. "Sarah? Are you Sarah?" she seemed kind. She suddenly appeared cheerful and introduced herself, "Hi, Sarah, my name is Patty. Crotchety told me to take you to the cafeteria and such."

I gave her a questioning glance.

"You know, Crotchety. She calls herself Nurse Crenshaw, of course, but I like to give some people names that are more appropriate. I think names should fit a person's character, don't you?"

Crotchety…is that all? I think I'd give her a much more despicable nickname after what she said to me.

Patty continued chatting as she attempted to help me up, but I was still weak and had to sit down again for fear of falling. "Here now, put your arm around my neck. You can do it," she said.

I felt too heavy to move and just couldn't.

"Maybe I should get you a wheelchair?" she suggested to me carefully, then conspiratorially. "They can be quite fun, you know."

I didn't want a wheelchair, so with all my strength, I managed to stand.

"Good job, Sarah. Just hold on tight. We'll be okay, I'm pretty strong."

After we walked out of the door and down the hall, I could feel a little of my strength return. We went into the bathroom where Patty helped me wash up. Afterwards, we continued down the wide hall heading towards the cafeteria. On the way, Patty talked non-stop.

"They tell me you've not been here too long. Nice place, huh? I've been here a little while.

She added, "My dad said that he's going to take me home soon, just as soon as he can arrange it."

I felt secure having Patty hold my arm. As she talked, I only thought about who this new person was who was helping me. She appeared to be a few years older than me, maybe fifteen or sixteen, I wasn't sure though. She was at least a head taller than I was and appeared to have a strong build, though slender. Her soft brown eyes were what fascinated me. They felt kind yet held a curious and mischievous twinkle. Dark, shapely brows accented them.

I put my hand to my own brows and rubbed them softly with the tip of my finger wishing I had dark brows like hers—mine are too light to even notice— and the way she pinned her black, wavy hair up on her head in a swirl reminded me of how Grandmother wears hers. I sighed as I thought about Grandmother. I missed her so much. I wondered where she was or if she was all right, but Patty's continuous, loud talking interrupted my thoughts.

"Anyway, let me tell you about some of our fellow inmates, as I call them," she went on.

Just then, we passed an open door. Inside was a short, older woman with brown and gray hair. She sat on a cot, motionless, staring at the floor. Her right hand moved nervously back and forth. Patty leaned in and whispered softly in my ear, "There's Catlady, short for Katherine. She's scary. I wouldn't talk to her. She yells at people that aren't around. Sometimes she sounds like a cat screaming in the night."

I recalled the screaming sounds from the night before and thought that maybe she had made those horrible noises.

"What she does is this: she looks up and yells as if who or whatever she's screaming at is standing high above her. Well, the point is you wouldn't want her to think that you were one of those invisible people. I've seen other people who live here get yelled at by her and run off crying. So stay away from her." Patty paused a moment then added quietly, "I thought of calling her the Screamer, but I don't think she really knows where she is. I mean she's probably mad at someone from a long time ago. She wouldn't understand."

I smiled at Patty's kind consideration of this scary woman. We continued down the hall.

"I wonder if Ratlady is in her room," she said peering up the long hallway. "Maybe, she's already terrorizing the cafeteria."

I quickly glanced at Patty in surprise and could tell she expected and enjoyed that response. She seemed to love the drama of this awful place, which almost made it bearable, at least for the moment.

"Well, let me tell you about Ratlady. I gave her the name a few months ago. Now just about everyone calls her that. She doesn't seem to mind. You see she is the person most aware of our other inmates, the rats. It is an obsession with her. She even sees them when no one else does. Of course, they are always twice as big and much fiercer when she sees them." Patty paused, adding, "Don't pay her too much mind when she catches one and shows you. She likes to do that, you know, by holding them by the tail. They wiggle like crazy!"

This gave me the chills.

As we slowly approached an open door that I presumed to be Ratlady's, Patty stretched out her neck and said clearly relieved, "Nope, she's already gone. Oh, well."

We continued down the long monotonous hallway and Patty talked about a few other characters. However, my mind began to drift. What she was saying sounded like a bunch of empty words until the wide doors opened before us, and she announced loudly, "Here we are." A bright flood of sunshine hit my eyes and I couldn't see a thing for a moment. When they adjusted, I saw the shimmer of green grass lit by the sun and glistening after the rain. My spirits lifted a little.

"I think we'll take the walkway through the grounds instead of the covered one. It's such a beautiful day!" she exclaimed. "I hope you don't mind."

The breeze on my face gave me a warm feeling inside. It was familiar and reminded me of home. The warmth of the sun pressed softly on my skin, and as I gazed up, I noticed big puffy clouds waltzing through the blue sky and leafless trees whose finger-like branches seemed to reach for life itself. With a big sigh, I stopped walking.

"What's wrong," asked Patty, "getting tired?" She glanced at a wooden bench situated under the shade of a large camellia tree. "Why don't we stop here for a moment?"

After we sat down, Patty immediately jumped right back up and picked two pink rose-like flowers from the tree. She then reached in her hair, pulled out a couple of bobby pins and fastened one flower to my gown and one to hers. "There now," she began. "We have something to remind us of how life is really beautiful."

Patty's animated gestures made me think she came from an Italian family. With her hands orchestrating every word she added, "Because, when we are inside, with all the strange characters and keepers of the characters, the beauty of life will be easy to forget, as I'm sure you already know."

I reached over to touch my flower, feeling its soft petals and to gaze on its beauty. I wondered how Patty knew so much about what was important in life. I studied her face shining bright in the rays of the sun and realized that she was pretty and soft as the flower. I became curious. Why was she here? How could she seem so happy, and how does she know how to cope in this awful place?

"What are you so puzzled about, Sarah?"

I sat silent for a moment, not sure what to say or if any words would come out that made sense. Patty turned her gaze to the trees and sky. Finally, some hard to manage words began to slip from my mouth slowly, "Oh...I don't know...really. I was just wondering...wondering well, you seem so normal and...."

Patty laughed and, with a mad look on her face, loudly proclaimed, "Yes! And so do the doctors and nurses!"

I found myself giggling at her joke, and then we were giggling together. "I will tell you sometime soon Sarah, I promise. But for now, we must get to breakfast before they stop serving, that is, if you can eat the stuff that they call food here."

Patty helped me stand up and we went on to the cafeteria that was right around the corner. Just inside the doors, staring eyes from strange faces observed us seemingly all at once. I glanced around and noticed that some women were talking aloud... to no one in particular.

"Who are they talking to?" I asked Patty.

"Oh," she answered shrugging her shoulders, "I don't know, maybe nobody ever listens to them or ever did, so I guess it doesn't matter to them if anyone is actually there or not."

Patty guided me around some of the long tables and then to the end of one that was next to a window. "You sit here," she told me, "and save me a seat. I'll go and get our food."

Patty walked off to wait in a long line next to counters that reminded me of our school cafeteria. Without warning, a sinking feeling gripped my heart and I suddenly felt abandoned and alone. But I remembered what Patty had said and I touched my flower, reminding me of our walk in the sunshine. Other patients began to stare at me. I thought right away that I must be a terrible sight. I had no idea what I looked like or the state of my hair for that matter. Using my fingers, I tried to comb through the straight blond strands. There were so many tangles there that I finally gave up.

Patty returned with a tray of food. It balanced two bowls of lumpy, cold mush, and two pieces of dried-out day old toast. Patty glanced at me with her spoon in her hand and produced an expression that suggested we were just about to embark on a dangerous journey. I took a sip of what was supposed to be juice, but was mostly water, and then crunched a bite of toast that was reminiscent of a wood chip.

"No one is going to get well with this kind of food!" she announced, then she whispered in my ear. "What I do is pretend it's home cooking. First, you have to close your eyes and imagine you're in your kitchen...that is of course if you had good food at home like I did."

I smiled at Patty and we both closed our eyes. I saw my kitchen and steaming food ready to take to the table. I used to love to taste everything and said that I was the chief food inspector. For the first time in a long while, I wanted to talk about something. Patty was fun to listen to and I began to feel as if I were back in school with my friends. When I finally spoke up my words tumbled out slowly, "I, I, can remember our wonderful food."

"What is your favorite?" Patty asked.

"Um, well, this mush sort of looks like Nan's terrinee."

What's that?"

I began slowly and hesitantly, "It's...rice pudding...and absolutely wonderful. Nan cooks it all night in the oven. In the morning, we have a thick crust on top of it that tastes like caramel." I closed my eyes to take a bite of 'terrinee'.

"By the look on your face, it sounds delicious. I think our cook forgot the recipe! Do tell me Sarah, who is Nan? And by the sound of it, are you French?"

"I was born here in Napa, but Grandmother was born in France. We had a French housekeeper, Nanette, I called her Nan."

"That's funny," began Patty, "my grandparents were both born in Italy, but my mother did all the cooking."

Patty's face appeared sullen for the first time. I wanted to ask her what was wrong and if it had something to do with her mother, but I was afraid to impose on her. Then Patty interrupted my thoughts.

"Tell me Sarah, tell me all about Nan."

Instantly, I smiled again.

"Boy, she must have been something, that's the biggest smile I've seen on your pretty face today," Patty complemented.

I grabbed a piece of my hair, and with a serious pout said, "I don't feel pretty, that's for certain."

"Oh, you just need a new hairdo," she said quickly and fiddled a little with my tangles. "You'll be pretty as ever. We'll do that later, I promise. Now then, tell me about Nan."

"Let's see," I began slowly, "Nan was Grandmother's cook even before I was born...I used to always go into the kitchen...and watch her. Sometimes, like when she was peeling vegetables, I'd sit on her lap and help. She is always soft like a big sofa. She isn't real fat or anything just," I paused to quote Nan in a French accent, "'plump like zee roasting cheeken' she used to say. She always made me smile."

"You do that quite well!" Patty exclaimed, "Do you speak French?"

"Not really. Nan said I did when I was two or three, but Grandmother insisted we speak English since we were Americans. And we did as Grandmother said."

"What about your mother and father?"

"Oh, I don't remember them. They died in a train accident when I was just a baby."

"I'm so sorry."

"That's okay. It's as if I have two mothers because Grandmother and Nan both raised me. Nan is more comforting, and Grandmother is more like a father only because she ran the business when Grandfather died. She is always occupied with business."

"Did you know your grandfather, Sarah?"

"No. He died, I think, in 1922 or '23. Grandmother said that he liked his drink too much."

I missed my Grandmother. A deep sadness filtered in, altering my mood. I crossed my arms in front of me and held my shoulders tight, not wanting to let go. My head rested upon my right hand and I began to rock back and forth. Patty continued talking, but I didn't listen. My only comfort was to hold myself tight and rock. I didn't want to let myself go—I won't leave me.

Patty put her arm around my shoulder and helped me up. Very quietly, she guided me to the courtyard outside and began to take me around the grounds. We walked under a row of trees near the edge of a tall cement wall. At first, I noticed only the change from shade to sunlight strike my eyes, but after a while, I began to see other women that were out here as well.

One sat on a bench curled up crying and nearby her an older woman walked back and forth yelling at an invisible foe up in the trees. On the other side, four women sat quietly on a long bench underneath a large tree. I watched them for a moment and noticed that they were not speaking to one another. As I scanned the courtyard, I realized that everyone seemed very sad.

I wondered if this is where they take all sad people. Maybe, if I was happy then I could go home. But I'm just as sad. Home, where is home? My mind feels like it's in a fog and I'm having difficulty picturing home. It seems so far away and feels like a different life or someone else's life.

Patty tried talking to me, but I didn't care to say a word. When we sat on a bench, I thought about her. I liked having her with me, but I just wanted to cry. That's all. Just cry.

The rest of the afternoon faded into nothing as if it didn't exist; yet it seemed certain to last forever. Patty didn't say much, or I didn't hear much. Empty time passed until I found myself back in my room, all alone.

It was cold, and the rain was back again, tapping on my window. I stared outside and watched the night steal the last of the day's light. I heard movement outside in the hall, but no one came in. A dim light rayed through the small window in my door. It beamed quickly through my room, as if it were scouring for something lost. First, it went to the corner of my cot, on the tall locked cabinet, and on part of the wall and then disappeared. Nothing else was in my room, but the barred windows and me.

My feet began to burn from the cold, and I curled up under the thin blanket, staring out the window at the starless night. All was now dark. I so wanted to sleep, to dream of a different life, to have pleasant dreams, as Grandmother used to say. But I was alone, and something felt wrong, terribly wrong. I began to cry.

Why am I here? What did I do wrong? Where's Grandmother? Why doesn't she come and take me home?

I finally drifted off to sleep only to fall right into the mare's grasp. With a jolt, I awoke screaming, bolting out of this awful, sickening dream. My body shook uncontrollably, and my senses scattered. Worse, the dream didn't fade but hijacked my mind, for what seemed an endless period of time.

Down a dark hall blackened by night, I walk slowly, feeling my way by touching the walls.

Someone or something is behind me. It tries to grab me, and I must run. Death is licking the back of my neck with a long, wet forked-tongue. I need strength to run away, but my body moves slower and slower. Every movement I make grows heavier with lethargy. I begin to sweat in my struggle, and the power of my will leaks out of every pore, vanishing completely. I have no strength to run. My eyelids close and I fall in slow motion. Round and round my head spins and body topples. I know I must open my eyes as my body hits the cold, hard floor—to run and hide from Death—but a terror, thick and oppressive, envelopes the hall and lies on top of my still body like a heavy blanket. I cannot move.

I heard my breath. It was shallow and fast. My eyes dart about. I noticed outside that the edge of the crescent moon was beginning to cast a soft light into my room. I stared at the glow and a familiar feeling arose within. I like the moon. The cool of the moon.

Faint at first, I began to hear other sounds in the night. I listened and realized that it was sounds of sobbing that echoed down the halls. Then, the haunting sounds of distant screams pierced the darkness. I thought of Catlady, Ratlady and other tormented souls like me crying out for comfort and help in the dead of night. Are they also stepping out of dreams, away from the mare's grasp? Are they as sad as I am?

While I listened to the strange voices—some screaming, some talking loudly and others sobbing—my own fears ironically began to fade. Inexplicably, my thoughts even changed. All this weirdness surrounding me has nothing to do with me, I thought. Suddenly feeling the difference between myself and these others,

I was mysteriously lifted above this place of terror, which I had just moments before occupied. I began to worry about my fellow inmates, as Patty called them. I wondered if their enemies were once real and now live on as haunting memories.

As this feeling grew stronger in my heart, I felt a need to run down the hall. This time however, I wanted to run towards others crying out, to embrace them and let them know they were not alone. Without any forethought or reconsideration, I lifted off my covers and stood with one hand on my bed until I found my footing. I know that this place offers very little comfort for tormented souls. I need to help the owners of the distant cries. I must!

In the glow of the crescent moon, I found my way to the door. I turned the knob and discovered that they locked it from the outside. My fist pounded on the door repeatedly. The thundering sounds, no matter how hard I hit, fell into empty space and joined the cacophony of the night. My body slowly sank to the floor.

A dog barked outside my window. I turned and then leaned up against the cold door to once again see the crescent moon peeking through clouds—hovering low and moving slowly—overhead, outlining them in a soft glow. Its soft rays poured through the bars casting long dark lines of shadow across my floor almost reaching my legs. I sat there, staring at the moon, watching it appear and disappear behind the clouds, and the lines appear and disappear like ghostly figures until the cold floor begged me to retreat to my bed.

As I lay on it, I held my pillow gently to my heart, as a mother would a baby. I thought about caring for the other inmates and my wish to help them and imagined that I was carefully tucking that desire into the folds of my heart where no one could find it. My eyes rested upon the crescent moon and as I cradled the warm feeling, I thought of Mary and Almighty God. "Dear God, I pray that one day my love, borne out of my sadness and fear, will reign gloriously to somehow help others...somehow, someday, someone."

The Castle Tower

The morning bell's constant ringing pulled me from a dream, the memory of which slipped easily through the fingers of my mind. I gazed out of the windows as my heavy eyes began to focus on the brightness of the day before me and at the treetops softly bending in the wind. Fragments of a dream began to filter back in, or was it a dream?

Images of an enemy locking me high up in a castle tower, unable to escape, brought an anxiety I could not ignore. Yet, I knew that someone was out there waiting to rescue me. I had to go to the window and signal to my savior that I was ready.

I slipped out of my covers onto the cold floor and walked across the small room anticipating my getaway. With my fingers pressing down on the windowsill, I scanned the outdoors. Beyond the bars, I saw sparse branches shaking from the strong breeze, chasing away the last leaves to join other leaves in a falling, fluttering cascade and behind them stood majestic and proud fir trees. However, no savior was in sight. Where is he?

I turned to my right and saw another building. It had many windows like mine, all in a row; each one covered with black bars. I realized it must be an extension of my building. Then, on my left, I saw more barred windows set high in a long wall. I pulled myself up onto the very tips of my toes and peered down. I saw the lawn, and then I remembered.

I am not high up in a tall tower. There is no castle, and no one will rescue me today.

"Hi, Sarah," said a man's voice startling me. Off my toes and onto the flat of my feet, I turned to see a handsome man with dark hair. He wore a white coat, clean and pressed. A clipboard rested perfectly balanced in one of his palms. He held a green fountain pen in his right hand, posed and ready for its next assignment.

"Feeling better?" he asked.

I wasn't sure how to answer this man. Something about his face brought a smile to me. I didn't know why. It was a kind face and I thought for a moment that maybe he might rescue me, and that maybe I was right about the tall castle tower and a savior after all.

"Come, Sarah, sit down here," he asked, indicating with a tilt of his head the direction of my cot.

I walked slowly, sat down as he required me and waited for him to speak but he just stood there. The only sound I heard was the scratching of his pen and my foot brushing back and forth against the cold floor. My visions of castles and towers vanished, as quickly as they first appeared. The room felt cold again and ominous, as if the air breathed a wicked tale yet untold.

"You seem stronger than yesterday," he stated matter-of-factly as he sat down next to me. He took an instrument from his top pocket, clicked on a light and pointed it right toward my eye. "Look straight ahead," he almost whispered.

The piercing bright ball of white moved slowly from my left eye to my right. It hurt, and as it did, my thoughts leveled down to the awful situation surrounding me. I felt like I was a prisoner in the bad dream, in that castle tower, and would never escape, even though I had prayed. I wanted to push it all away, the dream—including him—right out the door.

"You look just fine, Sarah," he said, patting me on the leg. "Now, I want to tell you about the treatments you will be having." He spoke this slowly, then waited for my response.

I just glared at him.

He tried speaking in a reassuring tone, "Now, now, Sarah, there is nothing to fear. You needn't worry, my dear girl." He placed his arm around my shoulder. "I will be giving you the treatments and afterwards you'll feel like a new young lady. I promise. He smiled and began patting my shoulder nervously. "Remember, I am a doctor not a dance instructor!"

Yesterday? Was it yesterday or another day? I felt lightheaded and weak. Yes! This is Dr. Brown, I remembered now. He was the nice one. Almost breathless, I began to plead, "Oh, Dr. Brown, I don't want any! I don't need any treatments, really, I don't. I just want to go home!"

He began explaining slowly—choosing his words carefully—as if I were a small child, "Well now, Sarah, you only had one treatment and that was two days ago. For these to be effective, I mean, for you to feel your best, you will be receiving a treatment about every other day now for six weeks."

I grabbed the starched sleeve of his white coat and exclaimed, "Six weeks?"

"Well, I mean, you'll get to a point that you won't even remember them," he explained, gently removing my clutching fingers from his coat. "They are not all that bad. Believe me; I wouldn't give you one single treatment if I thought it wouldn't help. Besides, they will be all completed before you know it." Dr. Brown quickly got up as if he'd said too much already. "I will see you in a while, Sarah."

I made a face at him—realizing now that he was not so very nice after all—as he stood by the door jotting something down on his clipboard. Just before he left, he glanced back at me, directly into my eyes for a few seconds, blankly. Absolutely no emotion registered on his face. Then, he turned and walked out.

His blank expression stayed with me, fresh in my mind's eye for a while. It was as if it meant something or he wanted to say something to me but couldn't. It was an uncertain, yet certain look. It left me without any understanding of his intention or purpose or consideration of my well-being. It filled me with unfathomable loneliness.

After Crotchety took me to the restroom and back again, I lay on my cot and clasped my hands tightly, praying that the doctor would forget me and not return. I could hear other patients out in the hall chatting on their way to the cafeteria. My hopeful feelings of rescue from the night before evaporated like my dream. Then, my thoughts went to Patty and I wondered where she was. Did they instruct her not to visit me today? I felt hungry too, but Crotchety told me that if I were good, I would eat later. My eyes darted around the room seeing nothing to hold my interest and I only felt more tension build in my empty stomach.

Dr. Brown's queer expression remained vivid in my mind. Even though he said that I shouldn't be, I was frightened. I was in a hospital not a castle. Aren't hospitals where we're supposed to get help? Doctors and nurses are supposed to take care of me, but no one will tell me the reason why I'm here.

I could feel my thoughts turning inwards like bullets from a repeating rifle. Am I sick? What's wrong? Maybe I did something wrong, terribly wrong? I feel like I did. I don't want to be here or be having these treatments. I want to go home. Where's Grandmother? Why isn't she here? She wouldn't let them do this to me. I know she wouldn't. Why am I here?

Tears welled, pouring from my eyes. "I don't want to!" I screamed. "I don't want to!"

Wrenching fear swallowed my heart whole and I held myself close, rocking back and forth seeking comfort that I knew was impossible. I squeezed my eyes shut as tight as I could and tried to stop crying. I wanted to push away the fear of what was before me.

Sounds of 'click-clunk, click-clunk, click-clunk,' echoed rhythmically down the hall. It drew closer and closer, louder and louder, and then stopped. My door swung open. I gasped and held my breath until my tears froze. I felt dizzy. A silver cart came in first, followed by a different nurse with red hair. On top of the cart sat a black box with dials and knobs. They're going to kill me, my mind screamed!

Dr. Brown walked in moments later. Registering no emotion and making no eye contact with me. He walked over to the cart and fiddled with the dials.

I curled up into a ball, but the nurse pried me apart and forced me to lie on my back, pulling my arms and legs down straight. Under the small of my back, she placed a pillow. It was uncomfortable. I tried reaching around. I tried to pull it away.

"No, this pillow will protect your back, dear," she said kindly while stuffing it back in place.

"Now don't move it."

Couldn't she see that I'd been crying? Didn't she care?

Dr. Brown, for the first time since he walked in, looked right at me. I reacted with a puzzled look. The nurse turned to the doctor. Did she await his explanation too? Was she as confused as I was?

He turned to her and said, "You look pale. Are you going to be able to do this?"

She took in a deep breath. "I should be all right," she answered.

"Sarah, I want you to lie still. The nurse is going to prepare you for this treatment," he said and then placed his large hand on my shoulder. "Don't worry, dear, this will not hurt you. It is going to make you well, and that's what we want now, isn't it?" His voice was calm, yet deliberate. After a moment, he added, "And besides, you won't remember this at all."

Why should I be doing something that I wouldn't want to remember? My soul begged for mercy, but my head nodded obediently. I just wanted to go home but they wouldn't let me.

She strapped my arms and ankles down tight and stuck something cold in my mouth. I don't want it there! I can't close my mouth! I can't breathe!

Dr. Brown wheeled the cart next to my cot, took some sort of headset and placed it over my head, close to my ears. He then put his fingers on the dials of the black box and said, "Okay, Nurse Bonnet, stand aside."

As soon as she stood back, millions of thoughts raced through my mind. In the few seconds it took Dr. Brown to turn the dial, layers of mixed feelings condensed into liquid anguish and flooded the vessels of my body. Inside I was screaming, No-o-o-o!

"Bzzzzzzt," went the low quick hum of electronic particles. Laced with a force unearthed from the cruelty of man, it seared right through my very existence, scrambling all my yesterdays and all my tomorrows. In that crack of a second, my body cinched, seizing all my limbs. The jumbled jarring of electricity raced helter-skelter through every pore of my face, neck, bottoms of my feet, the skin of my body and my whole inner being. I scattered everywhere, forever fragmented.

My body sunk, falling into vast emptiness, below the pain, below that moment, into a space where the memory of my torment could spread no roots and time has no place to be. I began drifting in… and then out… of this place with each gasping breath, sometimes falling and sometimes floating in a light-blue nothingness. I breathed in, quivered, breathed out and quivered. Time faded away.

Slowly, a vision began to appear enveloping me in a warm feeling, beckoning me to come. A golden light surrounded the vision and my heart reached into it. When the warmth imbued me, a form of what was once my life began to take shape.

I find myself back home. I'm finally home.

Pandora's Box Opens

Barbara sat on the couch, sheaf of paper in her lap and sheets in her hands, while I cleaned the kitchen, anxiously waiting for her to finish reading my first four chapters. She came over around nine this morning and I felt she should be nearly done. I still couldn't believe how quickly she offered to read my manuscript when we first met a few weeks ago.

The encounter happened while I was at Beer's bookstore peering through the metaphysical section for books about previous lives, seeking comparisons to mine, when I saw her. She had dark hair unlike my strawberry blond and stood by the section marked Literary Criticism. She was about my height. Even though she wore casual clothes, I sensed an air of elegance along with intelligence just being near her.

Earlier that morning I happened to be thinking about having someone that I didn't know read my manuscript for a fresh perspective and here was this perfect stranger who indicated, upon our introduction, that she might be interested. Why not officially ask, I thought? When I did, surprisingly, Barbara—for this was the woman's name—seemed quite excited about the prospect of helping.

When Barbara first arrived, carrying a large satchel over her right shoulder, Tara, our Cocker Spaniel, greeted her with happy barks. I had a tray of hot scones I was just bringing into the living room for us to enjoy when the doorbell rang. So besides being excited about our new guest, Tara was also awaiting crumbs drops.

"Not now," I scolded her.

After Barbara met Tara with kindly pats and smiles, I said, "It's so nice to see you again and thank you so much for offering to help."

"You too. I've been looking forward to this," she said peering around. "What a beautiful house you have. It feels so calm and welcoming. Indeed, your whole neighborhood is charming."

"Thanks. I often hear that sentiment. Yes, this house is very special." I replied, then added, "It was built in 1923."

I showed her into the front room and over by our green couch that faces the ten-foot wide multi-paned casement window. "The view is pleasant and that's where I wanted us to talk.

Through it you can see our large sycamore tree and an old camelia bush, showy now with its deep red flowers."

As we sat down, she commented on the lovely view and then looked up at the ceiling.

"My goodness. It's so high!" she exclaimed.

"Yes, I love how both this ceiling and the one in the dining room are different. I don't know if you can see from here," I said, pointing to the next room, "but the top of the dining room wall curves up to the ceiling whereas this one *angles* up. Every time I walk in here, I feel good," I said, comfortably. "It must be the balance between the two, though both ceilings are around nine feet high."

"It does feel good," she agreed and then asked, "You live here alone?"

"No, my daughters, Carissa and Lara and I moved in here with my mother, Yvonne, six years ago when I left my husband. We later divorced."

"Oh, I'm sorry to hear that."

"Yes, it was difficult, but being here with my mother is a blessing. She is such a caring and compassionate person." I paused, then added, "Also, I had been teaching art classes in my studio out back for four years before we moved in, so it was really a very easy transition for all of us."

"Do you still teach art here?"

"Yes. I'll have to show you my studio when we're done." I paused a brief moment, reconsidering, "Actually, let me show you right now."

"I'd like that," she smiled.

Barbara followed me into the dining room, noting my mother's grand piano angled in the center of the space. She asked, "Do you play piano?"

"Only a little. This is my mother's. My father bought it for her after they purchased this house in 1970. I had just graduated from high school, so I lived here about a year or so before I got my own apartment. My mother has a natural talent. I grew up listening to her play the music of composers like Beethoven, Chopin and Gershwin. She only had four years of lessons during summer breaks and outgrew a teacher each summer," I laughed. "They said that she knew everything they knew. The last teacher told her she could be a concert pianist."

"Was she ever?" Barbara probed.

"She got married, life became busy, but she played on her upright throughout my childhood." I paused a moment and added, "I feel that her soul *is* music."

We walked through to the breakfast room that has a built-in corner cabinet and small dining table. I then pointed towards the hall and said, "There are two bedrooms and the bathroom to the left."

Barbara looked surprised.

"I know, just two bedrooms. My girls and I shared one bedroom when we first moved in. I had a double bed and they have bunk beds. Now I sleep on the couch. It's a sleeper bed."

"Oh, that must be better."

"Yes, I like sleeping in there for now. Someday, I'd love to build an add-on upstairs. It's such a large attic, you see, and there'd be enough area for two bedrooms and maybe a bathroom."

We walked into the kitchen and I mentioned, "Thank goodness I updated this a few years ago. It had a green sink and orange Formica countertop from the seventies! A family friend helped me. It wasn't too difficult. He cut the new counter and did the plumbing, which seems to always take more time than it should."

Barbara laughed. "I remember those colors. They were very popular."

"Yeah, and don't forget the golden-wheat color. If you had all three, you were in style back then. Oh, speaking of which, we also tore up the rust colored shag carpet when I moved in!"

"My goodness!"

We walked through the back door and into my studio.

"Look at all the beautiful art!" she exclaimed, then as she was pointing at one of my student's paintings, said, "I could never do that."

"Yes, you could. As it turns out, I'm a very good teacher. Actually, I should say I'm more of an art-mentor. I help everyone through their art projects step-by-step—from how to pick what to paint, underpainting, mixing colors and how to use a brush. I also have a summer program where we go to parks and each student finishes an oil painting of a scene in one week."

"One week? That's amazing. Really," she said, simultaneously shaking her head in wonder and praising me.

"Thank you," I said. "I love teaching. Actually, this was originally my father's workshop. Unfortunately, he passed away when he was only fifty-nine."

"I'm sorry. That seems awfully young."

I looked around the studio reminiscing. "I remember so vividly that when I was just four, he was building full-sized cabin cruisers entirely out of wood. He built four on commission, one that was for us plus he built a speed boat for the family. In addition to him being an architect he loved his hobbies."

Barbara glanced at me, gently, and said, "You must miss him very much."

"Oh, I do. I learned a lot, though, by watching him. Anytime he wanted to do something new he would take the time to study whatever it was and then, he'd get it done. Besides fishing, hunting, building model airplanes from scratch— since he was a teenager—he also built furniture, a trail bike, a dredger for gold panning and learned to fly a glider not long after we moved here." I paused and then added, "He gave me the confidence to accomplish whatever I put my mind to."

I pointed to the wooden flat file, "He built that before I was born." I paused a moment then added, "I feel close to him out here."

Barbara smiled.

After we went back into the living room and sat on the couch, Barbara reached into her satchel and pulled out a notebook and pen while I went to get her water and tea to go with the scones.

Returning with the refreshments, I looked at Barbara as I sat down on the couch and felt suddenly moved to know more about her. "I've been going on and on about me," I said. "What about you? Have you lived in Sacramento a long time?"

"Yes, I think so. Let me see… It's been about eighteen years now."

"Where from?"

"Minnesota."

"You don't have an accent!" I said.

"That's because I wasn't there very long. I was raised in Southern California. We moved quite a bit," she said, pausing, as if she were about to say something else. I waited.

"Books are friends that I could always take with me. I loved going to bookstores wherever we've lived." She stopped, smiled at me and said, "Every time I'm in a new city, the first thing I do is find a bookstore."

We chatted a bit more and I repeated how happy I was to have her help, to which she smiled and nodded. I explained that I wanted her to read the first four chapters and then we could discuss it.

"Do you mind if I take notes or make suggestions on the manuscript? "she asked.

"Not at all."

"Oh, I also brought my notepad, is that all right?" she wondered.

I looked at her and smiled. "You are so prepared! Of course."

"Did I mention that I belonged to a writing group where we would edit each other's work?" she said, with a look in her eyes that suggested there would be more about her to rely upon than mere reading comprehension.

"No you didn't," I said, happily. "Is that why you agreed to read my book so quickly?"

Barbara responded with, "That's one reason. The other is that I'm very interested in your memoir of recalling a previous life. Sounds interesting."

"You'll soon find out if it is or not," I said, and then, "I think I'll leave you alone while you read. I'll just take Tara for a walk, then work in the kitchen. Let me know if you have any questions."

"Sounds good," she said, as she slipped a pair of glasses out of its case.

When I returned from the walk, Tara immediately laid down at Barbara's feet by the couch, and that's where I found my new friend, sitting there, glasses on, the pile of papers in her lap and the couple of sheets of writing she had in hand, with Barbara herself engrossed in the reading. Barbara didn't lift her head when she told me that she didn't mind Tara being there, so I walked off and busied myself in the kitchen. Every so often I'd look in until I could see that she was nearly finished with the section I'd given her and then, I eventually came to sit a little anxiously by her on the couch.

I gazed through the front casement window at the sycamore tree. The sun brightened its trunk and branches until fast-moving clouds cast ominous shadows on that evanescent, periodic glow. How appropriate, I thought. Today will be the first day that I will actually be sharing my story, which, after a few years of mind-boggling writing process, had finally been completed.

As Barbara turned to the last page of my first four chapters, I sat there anxiously awaiting her response. Did I relay the horror, the fear and grief as real as it was to me when that life first opened up to me?

Barbara's kind eyes looked up at me in grief.

"My God, Kerry. This sounds awful. Was awful. I can't imagine going through an experience like that, much less how you ever remembered it."

"You're right on both counts," I answered, recalling how it made me feel, then sighed.

"Bringing back the memory of that life was extremely emotional for me and writing it was even more difficult."

"Why do you suppose you remembered it?" she asked.

I looked at her with raised eyebrows, hesitating a moment and then answered, "Well, I've thought about that a lot. I now believe that since reclaiming that particular existence with such vivid detail—sometimes, I have to admit, with more detail than I remember of my early childhood from this life—I've come to the conclusion that I was supposed to have that experience and destined to recall it."

"How can you say that? There are many experiences I never wanted to have, and I know I didn't ask for," she said.

"I can't argue with that. Either way, whether there is a choice or not, once we've had the experience, we have to deal with it. I wouldn't want to be in that life again, believe me. I know. I hated what happened right down to the core of me."

"How did you ever find out about it anyway? Did you have hypnosis or dreams or what?" asked Barbara.

I sat back on my dark green couch and took a deep breath. I've told the story so many times, it seems as if everyone should know it by now. The importance of recounting what happened to me in my past life feels important enough to relay it again and again though.

Important for others to hear so that maybe they can learn from my experience, and important in the hopes that by recounting it I can someday be completely released from the horrors I've recalled.

I took a sip of coffee and began, "I was in Scientology in the mid-to late-seventies."

"I've heard of that," Barbara said, slightly put off. "Isn't it a cult or something?"

"Well, I didn't believe at the time it was and of course that's a matter of opinion—whether you're involved or not. I was young, in my early twenties and the sign of the times was about spiritual enlightenment. It was quite fascinating to me because the philosophy was based on Eastern religions, which I still enjoy learning from and a science that dealt with the psychology of the mind, both of which are still my two favorite subjects." I paused and thought for a moment about what to say, half listening to Barbara while she talked about similar groups she'd heard of.

"Actually, I'm a bit embarrassed to say I was even in Scientology," I confessed.

"Tell me why," she probed.

"It got such bad press. I had to defend it, even to myself. Plus, I became a very zealous follower" I said, thinking back. "I know what it's like to become narrow-minded in the guise of being wise."

"Yeah, but you were young," Barbara said, earnestly. "Youth are always trying to break into new territory...uncharted experiences, as if there's something new under the sun."

I smiled and said, "You're so understanding. It was more than that, though. I did things for the sake of the organization that I would never have done on my own."

"Like what?" she asked.

"I don't really want to get into it too much," I began, rolling my eyes downward and shaking my head. "That's a whole other story, but I did things like talk to people I didn't think we could help because I was told to. I worked well over sixty hours a week and was subjected to humiliation by my seniors and co-workers when I didn't get my stats up, or my production up, for the week."

"That sounds like the way many businesses operate today," Barbara said, half-jokingly.

"I guess you're right. I was paid sometimes, but as little as $5 a week. Very seldom did anyone even make minimum wage. It's embarrassing really. I do know that I was not paid enough to subject myself to the humiliation and stress for the sake of a cause. It really went too far."

"It sounds like it. By the way, isn't that against the law?" she asked, with an obvious edge to her otherwise pleasant voice.

"Not when you're working for a religious organization," I replied, disparagingly.

"That just doesn't seem right," she said.

"Well," I said, "*That* was over twenty years ago and at this point in my life I look at the whole experience as just that—an experience that I learned a great deal from. I could explain my opinions on Scientology and its organization in great detail, but I'd rather keep the experience in context with my past life story, otherwise we'd never get to it."

"Okay," she sat back. "I'll play along. How did being involved with Scientology help with your ability to remember your past life?"

"Great question," I smiled at her and gave her a 'thumbs up'. "I'll try to simplify what it is. Scientology has a very specific way of counseling: one-on-one with a trained Scientology counselor, which is intended to increase abilities. It even has a specialized term; auditing, which means; to listen. This is done by asking questions related to aspects of living, like communication, problems and guilt. It also has what's called Dianetic counseling, which focuses on being released from unwanted feelings. This is usually where people discover past lives and hopefully discover the root of their suffering."

"Huh...that's interesting. Seems to directly relate to your own past life based on what I've just read of it," Barbara commented.

"We're getting a little ahead of ourselves," I said. "But, yes, that's what I thought would be interesting. In fact, at the beginning, after being involved in Scientology for only a month, I quit. I became disillusioned with some of the things I'd experienced. But then I decided to try it again."

"Really? Why?" she looked at me.

"Because it held the lure of discovering who I was in a past life and I became intrigued. I thought that if I could find out who I was, I could also regain knowledge from that life. It was the mystery that beckoned me, and the possibility of recalling past lives. I wanted to know if there was truth in what they claimed," I explained.

"So, you stayed. So, what happened? I mean, when did you learn about *this* past life?" she asked.

"Actually, I didn't learn about my most recent past life, the one you just read about, until I discovered many other lifetimes."

"You did? How?" she asked. "My goodness, that must have been hard to keep straight."

"When I was in the counseling session, I was asked questions related to a particular unwanted feeling, emotion or pain and would talk about experiences in this life that came up. Sometimes, though, I was still bothered by whatever I was trying to release, and the counselor would ask if there was an earlier similar experience. That's when it happened."

"What?"

"Suddenly, there would be a picture, a memory with feelings attached, something I had never seen before *in this life.*"

"Yeah, but how did you know that it wasn't just your imagination or some kind of suggestion that they made to you?" she asked.

"It is totally subjective, except for the E-meter," I said. Barbara wrinkled her forehead. "What is an E-meter? She asked.

"It is a gauge," I replied, "that registers resistance on a small electric current, a galvanometer of sorts, similar to a lie detector. I held onto two cans connected to the meter, while the counselor watched the gauge and asked questions. Basically, it sent a very minute, thank goodness, amount of current that was able to measure mental resistance to that current. This resistance supposedly represented negative mental energy from painful experiences.

"That's bizarre, Kerry," she said. "You volunteered yourself to be attached to electrical circuitry...isn't that ironic?"

"Yeah, but without getting too technical," I went on, "when a person is recalling a negative experience the needle rises to the right on the dial and when they talk about the upset the needle falls to the left. The moment the person experiences a release from the upset the needle on the dial would show this by what was termed 'floating', sort of slowly moving to the right and left.

This was used in counseling to help the counselor know if they were on the right track and when to finish. Part of the process was to complete each session with a floating needle, which usually meant that you felt good."

"Okay. That sounds like it would be actually helpful," she commented.

"It was. Before the E-meter the counselors were trained to look at body reactions, like dilation of the pupil, but that proved to be too inaccurate. The E-meter, in my experience, is a great tool for showing which direction the counselor should take and when to end the session.

"By-the-way," I told her. "There was no hypnosis. In fact, hypnosis was considered to be bad because the thrust of the counseling was to bring memories up from the subconscious, into the conscious mind so that you could have a cognitive say over what you felt or thought. It was believed that hypnosis could plant suggestions into the subconscious mind."

"I know people that have been helped with hypnosis and that they swear by it," Barbara stated.

"I've heard that too, but frankly I'd rather feel refreshed and at peace because I really felt that way, instead of someone suggesting it to me. And, by the way, it's not the electricity itself but how it's used that matters. In the hands of an evil megalomaniac, like Dr. Cox, it can be a hideous weapon. In the case of these counselors, we were in much more considerate hands. "

"You've got a point," she said. "I never thought of it that way before."

"Anyway, I'm actually getting off the *point*," I stated and smiled. "In all my time with them, I had a few hundred hours of this type of counseling that took me into many, many past lives, none of which ever included my most recent one.

"That's surprising," she said.

"Let me go back. The first time I saw a past life was thrilling. It was like opening up a window and stepping into another realm. As if when you die, the passageway to that life quietly shuts and becomes invisible. This counseling was like having a magic key to open it back up."

"That's quite amazing. I was wondering," she asked, "do you remember your very first life?"

"An interesting question. I doubt I do or did. I remember being in a place that seemed to be before the physical universe and I thought at the time it was my very first, sort of, pre-concept. That image, I recall, was difficult to grasp. All I remember is white that had no depth, emptiness, and then the sense of beings discussing what to create. I found it difficult to see what couldn't be seen since my impression was that it was before the physical universe. My only comparison is this: existing in the exact center of all dichotomies."

"That's either way over or way under my head," she joked.

"I think you've got it!" I laughed. "See, you didn't even have to go through all I did to reach this great understanding."

"Don't give me too much credit. I really don't have a clue as to what you're talking about and it doesn't seem like anyone could, but I'll take your word for it." Barbara paused a moment and added, "That reminds me, isn't the first creation supposed to be a Word?" I nodded, thinking it was. "Well, if that's the case, there would be no words to describe what is before the Word."

Barbara glowed with her new understanding. I added with an analogy, "We'll call that the Great dance around Truth."

"Ha, ha, ha!" she laughed louder than I'd heard her before. "We're so good," she said, wryly, wiping a tear.

"Yes, we are, aren't we? I was going to say something else before your great enlightenment. Let's see...." I thought for a moment, then blurted out, "Oh, yes, I remember. Since Scientology, I've done quite a bit of thinking about the nature of time itself, so I don't know if there is really a 'first'. I think we, as spiritual beings do not exist in time, we just think we do. Time is an illusion—we're not." Barbara gave me a queer look to which I responded, "Let's not go there just yet." She nodded, and then looked at me seriously.

"Let me ask you this then: how do you know what you were recalling was real?" she asked.

"It felt real," I said with conviction. "Just as real as the only time my dad slapped my face—for lying to him. I'll never forget that."

"Yes, but there is lots of talk now about imagined memories being thought of as real, that they have the same impact," she argued.

"I'm certain not all that I remember from my past life was the exact experience, and yet that doesn't really matter to me. I'm not trying to prove anything. I'm not a scientist. I did, however, learn a great deal from recounting these memories, whether they themselves were real or embellished. Most memories are reconstructed histories of our experience. But often the lessons are invaluable. Isn't that what living one's *Being* is all about?" I asked without expecting a response—and I didn't get one, only a curious nod to go on.

"I can tell you this though," I continued, "the memories did have feelings attached to them. It wasn't just images or pictures. These memories included strong emotions. Many of the emotions I'd never experienced in this life. I learned a great deal from doing this inner exploration. By bringing these painful experiences up from the subconscious to consciousness, I was able to realize or understand where some of my present-day feelings of discomfort originated. Knowing the source of the feeling gave me power over it, rather than the negative feelings having power over me." I paused a moment, recalling some of my lives.

"What kinds of lives do you remember?" she asked.

"You read my mind," I laughed. "I was just thinking about that. Well, I can remember being on other planets, flying in spaceships, being in a completely different dimension, being different sexes, along with living in France in the late eighteen hundred's and in Chicago in the early 1900's."

"Wow! That's amazing. Who were you in Chicago?" she quickly asked.

I chuckled a little and said, "I had a more fancy-free life than the one you just read about, I can tell you. I dated men with wealth and frequented underground nightclubs. It was short-lived, but quite fun while it lasted." Barbara smiled and raised her eyebrows.

I added, "Before that one I was a man."

"Really?" she asked.

"Yes, I was a Frenchman in the late 1800's. I did have problems though," I said with a slight pout. "I was frustrated, unsuccessful, monetarily speaking, an artist who became addicted to absinthe. Since I had little or no income, I was forced to live with my sister and her family in Paris. Not exactly what most people commonly think or want to think a past life is all about. No, it was not at all glamorous," I laughed and shook my head. "I wonder why it is that I never remembered being someone important like Cleopatra or even more realistically since I am an artist, a famous painter like Michelangelo? No, I get to be a drunk and a barfly."

Barbara and I giggled. She added, "I probably had to be your sister and take care of you!"

"Thanks a lot. I knew you would be back. You still want to look out for me, don't you? Want to loan me five francs?" I joked.

"You never know, mon frère," she said, shaking in laughter.

"Do you want more coffee?" I asked, after we'd both settled down. "Yes, thank you." We stood up, as did Tara, and all three of us paraded into the kitchen.

Barbara looked up at me while I poured the coffee and commented, "This is so fascinating. I had no idea that when you wanted me to help you with your book, we would be talking about all this other interesting stuff."

"I'm glad you find it interesting. I suppose it depends on who I'm talking to as to whether what I've investigated may have any significance," I stated.

I handed Barbara her coffee and we walked back into the living room. "You know, I mentioned this before about how it must have been complex for you to have numerous experiences of your past lives like that. Was it a difficult process to see all these lives?" she asked.

"Not really. It's sort of like watching a movie, except it's *your* memory and attached to them are feelings. Also, the ease in which I was able to see, contact and access a past life increased the more I explored this almost secret adventure. Frequently, I found that I had greater intuitive abilities in other lives, especially the ones that predated recognizable history. More often though, the session would end upon recalling a tragic death and from the perspective of this life I would learn something from the tragedy."

"I don't know if I'd want to find out about deaths," Barbara remarked, grimly.

"Honestly, it really wasn't bad. It was more like getting a chance for a new perspective, to rearrange the order of importance of what happened back then, like seeing something in a new light. Actually, there was a physical change at the moment of this new understanding."

"What do you mean?" she asked.

"Well, any bad feelings or negative feelings would magically lift off. I could actually feel the negativity leave my body; and at the point of this release I'd feel great, almost intoxicated. I could go into session feeling normal, and a few hours later come out feeling enlightened and euphoric. My counselor would report, 'Your needle's floating.'"

"Sounds great. Where can I sign up?" she asked, humorously.

"Please, don't be so eager." I pleaded, turning serious. "On the flip side, it's not all that great; or I should say that there is a price to pay, and I'm not talking about the exorbitant cost either. Increased awareness comes with increased responsibility. Unfortunately, I found out that nothing is absolute. Scientology promised much more than it could deliver or had the capability to. This is my opinion, especially after I recalled my most recent past life."

"Why, what do you mean?" she asked.

"Rather than a window opening up to a past life that I could easily shut away or become released from, recalling my past life as Sarah was like opening an earthquake fault. It was no longer another life I could view from a distance, or an innocent flirtation with a novelty. My unearthed past life suddenly became part of this life, like it was never separate. The only difference was that I had two different bodies, two different birth parents. No, it was nothing to be elated about."

Barbara looked at me with surprise, and almost disbelief. I think that she saw me as strong, sure of myself and down to earth and wondered how I could explain this peculiar state I had gotten myself into. "Here I was, suddenly confronted with unresolved issues from a past life that were now just as much a part of me as the conditions of this life. To that degree, I had to resolve these issues on my own since I couldn't go back and talk to the people that I took umbrage with from another life. It has taken a long time to come to terms with this past life and it has not been easy. In fact, it has taken me almost twenty years since I first recalled it, to finally feel that it is mostly resolved."

"What do you mean *mostly* resolved?" she asked.

"For instance, I can talk about it now and not have haunting feelings drape over me like at first. Yet I know it's an aspect of me that will never resolve completely," I paused to think of an example. "Have you ever seen shows about people who suddenly recall being abused and sexually molested when they were children, and had blocked it from their memory?"

"Yes, it's disgusting what people can do to children," she said shaking her head.

"And how difficult it is for these people to untangle memories like that?" I asked.

"Yes," she considered, thoughtfully.

"Well, my life as Sarah was blocked from my memory. Not just because it was a past life, but because it was full of experiences no person in their right mind would ever want to recall. Now, I was faced with memories gushing forth that I had to somehow come to terms with and understand. It was like opening up a gate to Hell. I was unleashing memories that even in my past life I wasn't cognizant of. I had buried them back then because they were too horrific to face, and now they were suddenly flashing before me in one counseling session that lasted just two hours!"

Barbara began to riddle me with questions. "What happened in that session, when you first recalled that life? It must have been awful. What was the first thing you remembered? Did you ever get released from there?"

"Something I will never forget. I was in a session focusing on communication. It wasn't a Dianetic process where the questions were tailored to help transport one to an earlier time, it was a Scientology process. They were more like: 'What can you communicate with?' or 'What do you have difficulty communicating with?' That's when it happened."

"What? What did they mean by '*communicate with*'?" When, what happened?" she asked.

I answered by saying, "The year was 1977. My counselor, Suzie and I were in a small dimly lit room. I was sitting in a comfortable chair holding onto the cans," I explained this by putting my hands up in the air as if I were holding them.

"I was across a desk from Suzie. In front of her was her E-meter shielded by a long board so I wouldn't get distracted by the meter or her writing. It was so that I could concentrate on her questions.

"'What's happening?' asked Suzie.

"'I don't really know,' I had replied, and opened my eyes. I thought about it again. My body quivered. 'All I can feel is...I think I'm getting shocked or something.

"So, I looked over at Suzie, hoping for an explanation as to what was happening to me as this overpowering force seemed to invade my very soul, and I didn't know what to make of it. Suzie's eyes also shared my surprise, as I recall.

"'Okay,' she says to me, baffled. 'I'll ask the question again. What can you communicate with?'

"My body instantly shakes uncontrollably, deep from within when she asked that question, and I told her I didn't know. I just felt this jolt running up through my body. I remember shaking my head and repeating 'I don't know.'

Barbara interrupted with, "Did she check the meter? Were the volts too high?"

"No," I said. "There's no adjustment like that. It was the same as usual."

"So then Suzie told me, 'I'll ask the question again,' she had spoken this very softly. 'What can you communicate with?' Before she even finished with the question, a jolt of energy ran up and down quickly through my body again. There is no visual memory to go with the feeling. I can't see where I am, who I am and I began to feel anxious, as if I had to come up with something, and I was compelled to answer the question. "Maybe, I was shocked to death or something. Maybe, I got the electric chair!" I nervously joked, but then I soberly added, 'I've never felt this sensation before.'

"As I spoke about the jolt of energy, I noticed Suzie glancing down at her E-meter. Her head reared back; she stared at me, eyes wide, which told me that this memory had registered more energy than she had ever witnessed in all her counseling. I think again about the question she'd asked and again I feel the same rush of disturbing energy zip through me.

"'Okay," Suzie began again patiently, sending me one of her reassuring smiles. "I'll ask you again: What can you communicate with?'"

"'I think I'm being shocked, but I don't see anything,' I answered.

"Suzie tried to finish the process of questions, but I had tapped into something more powerful than I had ever witnessed before. It didn't just release. It did not go away and forced us to take a different approach.

"Being well-trained, she quickly surmised what to do. After a short discussion, we both agreed to take a detour, however long and necessary to use a more suitable process: a process that would help me unravel this powerful memory which had proven to be not merely an interesting flirtation with a former life.

"'When was it?' she asked me.

"'1938 or '39, I think. Yes, 1939.' I answered. This surprised me because never before, in all my counseling, had I come across a life that close in time to this life. I didn't know why the date emerged.

"'All right," she went on, 'what is the length of the incident?'

"'A few years,' I answered.

Barbara stopped me: "A few years?"

"Yes," I answered her.

"How could you be shocked for a few years?" she asked, doubt registering in her eyes.

"Well, the incident of that first shock treatment itself occurred during one particular day, but I found out that there were so many terrible experiences I had had at that hospital—experiences after that particular shock treatment, plus experiences before I ever arrived there. Somehow, because of the intensity of the traumas they bunched up together like in one big ball, which made it a very difficult process and for me to unravel."

"I wouldn't doubt that," Barbara stated with alarm and an empathy that quickly dispelled her disbelief. "What happened after the shock treatment? I mean, you were okay. Right?"

"I don't know about being okay," I looked at her. "I wasn't dead—not yet, anyway. But I will tell you that I didn't realize until much later that this opening, this sudden exposure of my previous life, was my own Pandora's Box opening up. Once it was open, it would not shut."

Barbara looked at me with such compassion, that I actually teared up. "That sounds so frightful. When you say, 'Pandora's Box' what exactly do you mean?"

"Let me open my dictionary and read it to you." I grabbed it from the coffee table and quickly thrummed through the pages. "Here it is. It says, 'The god Prometheus stole fire from heaven to give to the human race, which originally consisted only of men. To punish humanity, the other gods created the first woman, the beautiful Pandora. As a gift, Zeus gave her a box, which she was told never to open. However, as soon as he was out of sight, she took off the lid, and out swarmed all the troubles of the world, never to be recaptured. Only Hope was left in the box, stuck under the lid. Anything that looks ordinary but may produce unpredictable harmful results can thus be called a Pandora's box.'"[i]

"Yes, you definitely opened that box!" Barbara paused a moment then said, "I'm curious. You've mentioned how, in some ways, recalling this experience affected your life afterwards, but what about how you felt when you first opened the Pandora's Box, as you've labeled it? Didn't it freak you out?"

I looked at her with surprise. She was asking me something I hadn't even thought to address with her.

I can picture it as if it were yesterday and as I did, I realized how much that moment has been seared into my memory. I felt my eyes feeling puffy. I began with care, "It was quite horrific, Barbara, really. I've looked at it so much that I'd almost forgotten the degree of suffering I felt."

"What happened?" she demanded.

I stopped a moment as I looked back. Sighing, I took a deep breath and continued, "The moment Suzie asked me 'When was it?' I began crying more than I ever had in my entire life, more than I even thought possible and have never cried like that since. I'm not one to cry, but tears simply gushed out, like an open artery. They just couldn't stop."

"What thoughts passed through your mind?" Barbara pressed on.

"To be honest, I couldn't think. I was so afraid," I paused a moment realizing what I had just said. "I hadn't thought of it like that before. The grief felt eternal like it would never go away." I looked up at Barbara, then continued, "That moment tapped into a well of sorrow I could never imagine possible. It was as if no matter how much I cried it would never be enough. I couldn't stop. I had no choice. Suzie repeated the question over and over in what seemed like an eternity before I was able to answer."

Barbara had so much compassion showing on her face that I teared up again. She put her hand on my knee and gently asked, "Then what?"

"When I was finally able to determine the year, the grief lifted enough to continue. However, I felt shell-shocked from the grief itself."

"I don't know how you managed it, Kerry."

"Actually, "I told her, "at some point—not clear about exactly when—I eventually internalized what was happening, almost as if it didn't matter. After all it was another life, I rationalized. At least that's what I kept telling myself."

"I understand why you'd want to think that way," she commiserated. "But, clearly based on those first chapters that I read, you got back to it. So, how long did it take for you to see everything from that life?"

"It took three weeks of almost daily sessions until I came to enough of a release and understanding to get on with my life." I paused, but then added, "I do have to say that I am happy I faced that life with the help of Suzie. Just that alone, that *facing so much evil* and knowing the truth, helped me know my own courage. However, I knew deep inside there was more to the story." I paused again and then went on, "In hindsight, I believe now that I was supposed to handle it on my own. It took another twelve years and changes in my life before I was ready though."

"What about now? You mentioned that it is 'mostly resolved'," she quietly asked.

"I don't know. I just keep pressing forward. All I know is that when I pay attention to my heart there is something in the core, like a sliver of an open wound, and I can feel pain and sense an energy that is still there. And no matter how much I immerse myself into Sarah's experiences and document what I recall, it feels irreparably broken. Much better, but still not whole."

I hesitated a moment then added, "But I persist and hope. All I can do is hope."

"I'll pray for that too," said Barbara.

"Thank you. Thank you for being here and thank you for caring. I really appreciated it." I held back tears.

We hugged. It was a warm hug. A needed hug.

I sighed and sat silent for a moment while contemplating all the harrowing events I had yet to tell, then thought about my next section. I know that no matter what, I have to continue on this path. I checked my watch and asked, "How much time do you have?"

"Let's see," she said glancing at the clock, "I have a few more hours."

"Really? That's great. I have the next part ready for you, if you don't mind. It's Sarah drifting back in time before being hospitalized."

"That's right. I remember, "she said, gazing off at the window and the sycamore tree.

"It's not too long. Then maybe we could go over your notes from today?" I must have looked desperate as I said. "You wouldn't mind, would you?"

Barbara smiled, "Sure. Sounds good. I haven't anything major scheduled other than this today"

I reached over to the side table, carefully picked up the stack of the next several chapters and smiled as I handed them to her. "I'll just be in the other room, so let me know when you're done."

She nodded and grabbed the stack.

Barbara took in a deep breath (I'm almost certain that she must have been thinking in part, what have I gotten myself into and at the same time knowing their happenstance meeting meant more than mere coincidence).

The Party

Curled up on my window seat I read again, for the tenth time, my words

The warm breeze enters my open window carrying the sweet fragrance of fruit trees in bloom, bringing a smile to my face. Pink flowers and white flowers drape several trees reminding me of wedding cakes. I love my view from here! Second story windows always make me feel important somehow.

I imagine that I am high up in *a castle tower*, which happens to be the tallest tower in the castle, and that my room has windows on all four sides. Soft and warm burgundy velvet drapes cascade to the floor, frame each window. The red sandstone walls glow from filtering sunlight.

I look out at the mounds of earth as they transform into the hills of Portugal with their majestic castles, the ones I just saw in a National Geographic magazine. I can see the treetops for miles. I can see the nearby church steeple and the taller mountains in the distance.

Barking dogs and a church bell's distant chimes bring me back home, away from my adventure. I hear loud tin pops and glance down into my neighbor's yard. Jimmy's there, throwing rocks at cans neatly propped up on the fence. *I think that he's silly. I have no idea why he has a fascination for hitting cans. He says it's to practice for the fair and that he wants to win prizes and that it helps him throw better for baseball. I think he just wants to show off! He knows I see him from up here in my 'tower'. Every so often, and only when he knocks down a can, he glances up at me. I don't understand him, though. We used to play all the time, but now he doesn't pay attention to me, especially at school. Nan says that boys do that when they like you. I think that's silly. But I wonder....*

"Sarah, Sarah," Nan calls up the stairs. "Are you ready, mon chère, for the dinner party? There will be dancing."

Is it that time already? I shut my diary so fast that it makes a loud snap and then I run to the top of the stairs. "What is it, Nan?" I shout.

"It is time to get ready," she says.

"I'm coming!"

My mind races as I walk to my window. First, I have to put my book away. Who is going to be there? Oh well, I have to get busy.

I crouch down in front of my window seat, carefully pull back a narrow board on the front facing and place my diary inside. After securing the board, I peek out my window to see if Jimmy is still hitting cans, but he's not there any longer.

I pull out my light blue dress and matching white hat and gloves, which I've readied for the occasion and place them on my bed. Next, I get out my shoes and smile. They came with five different colored ribbon ties that I can interchange. The blue one matches perfectly. I straighten out the ribbon and feel its ribs between my fingers. I giggle because my fingers tickle.

I sit on my bed, lace up the blue ribbon, and then dress in front of my tall standing mirror. I spin about in a series of twirls and curtsy elegantly before my reflection. *This dress will be too small soon enough the way I'm growing! Just in time for our school-clothes shopping trip to San Francisco!* I smile, grab my hat and gloves and start out the door, then run back to the mirror for one last glance and twirl. *I love blue!*

"How pretty you look!" Nan exclaims as I bound down the stairs.

"Thank you, Nan. You really think so?" I ask, cinching the gloves to fit smoothly down my fingers.

Nan assures me as usual, "Of course, mon petite."

"Nan, I was wondering...?"

"Oui?"

"Do you think that you will ever lose your French accent? I mean some people do."

Nan looks at me quizzically.

"Well, Grandmother and you came from France about the same time, right?" I ask.

"Oui," she answers.

"Then, how come you speak more French than she does, and she doesn't have much of an accent at all?"

I had wanted to ask that for a long time and was always afraid to, but for some reason it finally blurts out, almost on its own! I study Nan's face to see if I hurt her feelings, but she seems to be thinking about what to say. So, I wait and keep quiet.

"My dear," she begins, "everyone is different. For some it is important to blend in and accents make them stand out. For others it is not so important." She pauses in thought a moment, then continues, "You see, speaking French reminds me of Sarlat and my friends and family that are still there. It helps me to be with them even though I'm here."

"How...?" I start to ask. But just then, Grandmother walks in. She is wearing the crème lace frock that falls to mid-length and gold-toned heels. Her silver and black hair carefully bound by a netted gold barrette is coiffed in a coiled chignon. Elbow length gloves gather along her slender arms. This may seem surprising, but she is both thin and dramatic, the height of grandeur. No matter where we go, everyone admires Grandmamma for her style and grace.

"Shall we leave?" She asks. When Grandmother asks, it's not a question but more a suggestion that we wouldn't challenge. She is always early to these events and detests the phrase, "Better late than never". As she strides by me, I stand tall in my blue dress ready to scurry off behind her.

As the door opens, the sweet smells of spring greet us. The sun is not yet down, and the red glow has just begun. A gentle breeze touches my face. A mysterious, yet familiar feeling overcomes me. It's as if I had these feelings from the beginning of time. I feel that I am a part of everything, the trees, the sky, the sound of the distant train whistle. I glance down at my arm and watch goosebumps rise. *That's strange. The night is warm.*

Mr. Frank, our driver, collects us at the gate beyond the garden in his shiny black sedan. He has always taken us to our social occasions and the many trips to San Francisco. Sometimes, when Nan is too busy to drive, he'll even take us on errands.

First, he opens the door and helps Grandmother in. Next, he escorts me to the other side, opens the door and I mimic her by giving him my gloved hand. A very slight grin appears to develop on his face. I smile and thus, properly escorted, slide into my cool, soft leather seat. Mr. Frank takes the driver's seat and we speed away.

Mr. Frank has never talked much. I've tried to carry on conversations with him many times, but his answers are so short the conversation is over before it has begun! I know he has a wife because he wears a wedding ring. For some reason, I feel bold enough to ask, "Mr. Frank, I was wondering... what is your wife's name?"

Grandmother immediately gives me an air that I am being very rude by asking him a personal question. However, Mr. Frank quickly responds, "April." Since I can no longer ask questions, I will just wonder and speculate about our perennially mysterious driver.

My deduction begins. He always has his dark hair trimmed short in the back—the part I see the most—and combed neatly on top. So, he must go to the barber often. I bet the barber, even though he likes and respects him, doesn't know much about him either. I imagine that his wife, April…. Then, without thinking I lean forward and blurt out, "Mr. Frank, can you wish her a happy birthday for me, please"

"Certainly," he says.

I purposely ignore Grandmother's glare and fall back into the seat to continue my imaginings. They have no children. They always wanted one or two, but it never happened. I can see him reading a book every night in his club chair and probably… no, I think he must smoke a pipe when he relaxes because there is always a slight perfume of sweet tobacco on his black suit, just like Grandfather used to have. They go to the beach on vacation—he always returns with a tan—and has a pleasant time. His wife is soft spoken; I can't imagine him with a gruff wife, and I bet she too doesn't even know very much about him! Like me, she probably tried but realized it wasn't important. After all, Mr. Frank is always on time, never smells of alcohol, and is very courteous, so, no matter what, she stands by him.

Perfectly satisfied having gotten all my 'answers', I relax and enjoy the trip.

The familiar ride to the resort takes about half an hour. Along the way, we zigzag down small tree-lined roads passing by orchards, vineyards, and the famous chicken ranch (featuring white leghorns, my favorite). Upon our arrival, the maître d' escorts us to our table out on the veranda. We pass by other tables, all with lightly starched white tablecloths draping each table, posed napkins await and small vases of brightly colored flowers congregate in the center. When we arrive at our table, we see wine glasses arranged along with two elegant bottles of Cabernet Sauvignon—one of Napa's renown vintages. Grandmother always calls ahead with her choice of wine for the evening festivities.

Twinkling lights strung from pole to pole softly illume the tables. We sip our wine and watch the orange glow of dusk fade, giving way to an indigo background with tiny stars beginning to flicker. Soon, the tables fill with businessmen, officials and their ladies or wives, along with children and young adults, usually by train and then cars that come from the San Francisco Bay Area.

One after another, her friends and associates come to our table to visit for a while. Each time she gives them her hand and they sit down to discuss all manner of things from politics to vineyards and the weather. If need be, she always makes it a point that I am greeted. And I am just as she is, met in a dignified manner. Guests seldom forget once told. That is how important Grandmother's influence is.

There are also lights strung from pole to pole that frame the wooden dance floor where a small band is playing popular music. Several people waltz around or kick up their heels, recalling to me parties Grandmother talked about that took place in the past—wild parties during Prohibition—but now the parties have become more refined. I can't imagine her any less refined than she is around me, naturally.

I sit up tall in my chair, emulating her and take a sip of my watered-down wine. Someday, I will be an important figure, like her. Someday, I will have all manner of friends and acquaintances and will host parties where everyone will feel at home. Someday.

"I'm so full," I say and then sigh.

She gives me a scornful glance.

"I mean to say, I have had quite enough, thank you."

She places her hand on top of mine. "Why don't you go and dance with your friends?"

"You should dance too, Grandmother."

She smiles, and carefully wipes the corner of her mouth with the starched white napkin., "Right now I have some things to discuss with Dr. Simpson. You go ahead, my dear."

Her odd stare took me a moment to understand and then I realized that her knee must be hurting. Oh, dear! I almost embarrassed her. Well, on second thought, maybe not. She is not embarrassed that easily.

Dr. Simpson leans forward now, very attentive to what she wants to discuss. He really isn't a doctor, or I should say a medical doctor. I've been told that he is a PhD not an MD. Grandmother said that he is a professor, or at least he used to be. Sometimes though, I wonder if she can really understand his kind of 'philosophy' because it makes little sense to me!

I see my friend, Ann, near the dance floor. She's in my class and is often at these parties with her family. I excuse myself, but Dr. Simpson and Grandmother are already so thoroughly engaged in a discussion about the war brewing in Europe that they don't even pay attention to my leaving.

Ann and our friends are practicing the old-fashioned flapper dance with wild abandon out on the lawn near the stage. As soon as I walk up, she grabs my hand and insists, "Sarah! Come on! Join us!"

I try to match Ann's enthusiasm to the beat of "Ain't She Sweet". After we kick out our heels in unison, our hands fling up in the air, wildly fanning back and forth. Then, we bend down, pass our hands back and forth—just grazing our knees that knock together repeatedly—until we both are holding our sides laughing too much to continue.

The band announces, "Mood Indigo". I straighten my back and look Ann square in the eyes.

We grasp each other's hands, take on a more serious, open stance, and wait. The music begins.

Ann manages to take the lead and our once frenzied dancing slowly becomes refined. We imitate the older dancers as they waltz and spin gracefully on the dance floor and exaggerate by arching our backs and tilting our heads way back, so much so that if we didn't have a hold of each other we would end up on the grass! *This is too much fun!*

As usual, we stay very late, even after the band has packed away all their gear and left. I don't remember the ride home since I fall fast asleep as soon as I enter the car. I dimly recall that Mr. Frank was kind enough to lift me out of my seat and carry me all the way upstairs where Nan took over, helping me undress, even hanging up my clothes—something she usually insists I do. But she knows that if left to my own devices, I would probably end up sleeping on the floor in my party dress.

Snuggling up in bed, I watch the crescent moonbeams flood through my window casing, shedding streams of soft light over my coverlet. The sounds of the evening: people talking, laughing and music playing is waltzing through my mind while I drift off into the night.

Early the next day, the thundering engine of the tractor nearly deafens me. Roberto yells back from the driver's seat and I can't make out what he is saying...again.

"What?" I yell in his ear.

"When we get back, I want to show you the plans!" he screams.

I nod exaggeratedly. For more than an hour now, we have been doing what the adults call "surveying" of the newly cleared land for a vineyard of Cabernet Sauvignon grapes. Yesterday the rows scheduled for planting were carefully marked out in the freshly tilled soil. We would stop often and gaze at the slopes of the hills and Roberto would talk about 'shaving' the earth as a sculptor would clay. I always thought of Roberto as an artist of the land and that his clay was raw earth. Year after year, I see him transform what were simply hills and valleys into beautiful, perfect rows of vines that stretch for miles. The virgin plot we have been surveying will grow vines that came all the way from France just a few weeks ago and have been waiting patiently, as Roberto says, 'to be planted in the full California sun'. Ever since I can remember, Roberto has taken me out on his tractor into the vineyards. He says it's because he likes to see me smile from ear to ear, but I think he just wants to see me covered in dust!

As we head back, I find myself thinking about how we have managed, Grandmother and me, to save our vineyards when many other businesses failed during the Depression. She would always say, 'Even in the worst of times everyone likes a glass of good wine.' Of course, it's easier now than a few years ago. We, like others, were careful with our money; we managed better than most and would often invite old friends and new ones to big Sunday dinners. Sometimes, I thought our dinners were like Christmas to them. I imagined that they must not have eaten all week or hardly at all, as they left nothing on their plates! In the kitchen, Nan always clucked like a hen about having to feed everyone, but I noticed that beneath her stern expression was a little grin when the guests complimented her for her wonderful cooking.

In a few weeks, we're going to have another big dinner. This time it is to celebrate and bless the new vineyard. Even the Bishop will be here! Nan spends extra hours planning for his visit, organizing menus, starching and ironing linens, barking orders to the gardener. I know that she will eventually need my help too.

Roberto extends his hand to help me up and off the back of the tractor. I jump down hard, on purpose, sending up a plume of dust. He steps back abruptly, brushes off his pants and gives me an air of mockery.

"Gotcha." I say, grinning up at him.

He smiles.

On the way to the office, Roberto takes me by the nursery to see the new vines. Bundles of grapevines lifted out of the shipping boxes had the moist moss already shaken off their roots. After that, they were plunged into five-gallon buckets of water and large wash tubs. The water protects the delicate parts of the plants. When planted, the moisture will help stick the freshly tilled soil to the tiny roots. Soon they will get their wish, to be able to bask in the full sun.

The office has a large wooden table with edges that are smooth and worn, made from planks harvested from an old sailing ship. I always imagined what it might have been like to sail across the sea, standing on these very planks, swaying back and forth on the waves (which is why I got caught standing on top of the table too many times). Now, atop these planks are the plans for the new vineyard with rocks from the tilled land holding down its corners.

Roberto walks up to the table quietly and points out where we drove on the map. He notes changes on the plans that we discussed while we were surveying.

Then he consults my memory about what we'd talked about, which makes me feel grown-up. Then I realize that he just needs my recall to reinforce his own.

A distant sound of tires popping over gravel comes closer. Then stops. *It must be Grandmother!*

Soon she walks in without saying a word. We glance at her every so often and wait. She studies the plans and the changes Roberto noted down and then says, "Now, Roberto, you know that these vines have to finish being planted by early May?"

She is so silly. Everyone knows that!

Roberto humors her as always. "Of course. The skilled workers will be arriving tomorrow as planned."

Even though she doesn't raise her voice, her tacit airs make demands that no one would dare challenge. Today is no exception. Respectfully, Roberto waits for a reply. Her long fingers slide slowly across the plans as if her touch creates the magic spark necessary for the vines to produce. Once she is done, she looks straight at Roberto, nods, and begins walking out to Mr. Frank and her waiting car. I know that I am to follow her just as Roberto knows what he's supposed to do. That's just the way it always is. Grandmother is the master of silent expectations.

A Morning Song

W hen I hear the roar of a distant tractor, I think of Roberto. If it were up to me, I'd rather be with him, helping plant the grapevines today. But here I am walking to school, lugging books instead. I do hope all his workers arrived safely today, just as he promised Grandmother.

I love looking at the crisp blue skies, puffy white clouds and colorful blooming trees, and proclaim in my heart once again that this is my favorite time of year. Their fragrance reminds me of entering the perfumery in San Francisco where they have so many scents. The last time we went there, over a year ago, Grandmother bought me a tiny bottle of lilac perfume, but I used it all up already. Suddenly, I recognize my favorite scent and begin searching until I find it—a lilac bush. *Oh, how I wish I had another bottle of lilac perfume.*

I see my school in the distance and begin thinking about all the festivities coming up before Easter Break. We have a pageant on Thursday and we're off on Good Friday, plus all of next week! Since I'm in 5th grade, we get to decorate eggs and organize an Easter Egg Hunt, along with the sixth graders of course, for the younger elementary children after the pageant.

Pageants always make me feel nervous, but at least this year I can wear a normal dress, sing in the choir and not run around in a bunny outfit! *How embarrassing that was!*

"Sarah!" Jimmy yells, startling me. He runs to catch up. "You want me to carry your books?"

I just stare at him. "No, silly."

"Are you going anywhere for Easter?" He proceeds, undaunted. "We are. We're going to Los Angeles! We're going to see my Grandparents."

He pauses and continues rather dramatically, "This may be the last time. I think they're getting old and...."

I interrupt, "They can't be that old!"

"All I know is that Grandpa is having some kind of heart trouble. I heard my parents talking all about it."

I gave him a 'shouldn't be eavesdropping' look.

"Well, they thought I was asleep. Anyway, we get to go to some big movie houses!"

"Movie houses!" I begin to share his excitement. "Wow! Maybe you'll see some movie stars...and get autographs!"

Suddenly coy, he says, "Would you like me to get you an autograph, I mean, that is if I see any stars?"

I smile, "Oh, Jimmy...that would be *real* nice. Oh, that would be swell!"

Suddenly in my imagination, I see a big screen, bigger than any screen I'd ever seen, and all my favorite stars are there, one by one, they begin to appear:

Cary Grant,

Loretta Young,

Gary Cooper,

Bette Davis,

William Powell,

Myrna Loy...I love Myrna Loy. She's so funny.

Clark Gable,

Carole Lombard,

Jimmy Stewart....

In my reverie I suddenly sigh, "Jimmy...."

Jimmy's voice cracks as he manages to ask, "What?"

"No...um, I mean, well...do you think, uh, were you by any chance named after Jimmy Stewart, the most fabulous and famous star of film and screen?"

Jimmy shakes his head and manages to squeak out, "No."

"Well, did you know that he used to do magic tricks when he was little?"

"No."

"And did you further know that he was friends with Henry Fonda? And they went off to Broadway together?"

"No."

"Geez, don't you know anything about him?"

He becomes huffy. "No! Anyway, *you're* the one that reads all those magazines. You know so much about Jimmy Stewart, but do you know anything about Bette Davis?"

I roll my eyes. "No...do you think you might at least be able to get his autograph when you go to Hollywood?"

"Who said anything about going to Hollywood?" he says. "We're going to my grandparent's house in Orange County."

"But Hollywood is where all the movie stars are, silly. You can't expect to get autographs unless you're in Hollywood. Everyone knows that," I point out.

"Geez, I'm sorry I even brought it up!" He turns, on the verge of darting off....

I grab his sleeve. He spins and glares at me.

"Jimmy," I say, opening my eyes as wide as Bette Davis, batting my eyelashes...one, two, three times. "Jimmy, oh Jimmy, won't you please...try!"

He gives up. "Oh, all right already! I'll do my best."

Mumbling under his breath, I hear him say (while escaping my clutches), "But I'd rather get an autograph from the real Bette!"

I watch Jimmy walk away and notice suddenly that he seems taller. Even though Jimmy is a year older, we were always about the same height and now I have to tilt my head back to talk to him. I glance down at the back of his cuffs and confirm. *Yes, he's taller and I think he needs new trousers!*

It's Tuesday afternoon and I'm off to market with Nan and to the Bruning farm for eggs. Not only do we need eggs for decorating at school on Wednesday, and our own Easter, but we need eggs for the Easter Brunch that Grandmother is hosting. Each year she has a big feast and egg hunt to help raise money for the orphanage. It's so much fun! I get to paint one egg gold and hide it in our garden. Whoever finds the egg wins a fancy picnic with their family at a surprise location and they get to ride in the parade that afternoon. To raise money, each family donates to participate in the Egg hunt and gets a chance to win. There are also other prizes donated by local merchants.

I love to decorate the eggs. I usually invite friends to come over on Saturday and we decorate at least six dozen. Nan taught me how to decorate eggs when I was six and every year since then I teach new friends. We blow the insides out of the eggs first—so they won't spoil—and then decorate with wax and color. Those eggs also win prizes! The rest of the eggs are decorated more simply, not blown out and are for eating... before they spoil.

I enjoy staring out the window as we whiz by all of the symmetrical orchards on our trip. I scan the rapid succession of rows quickly appearing and disappearing and try to look down between the trees all the way to the other side of the orchard. I'm not sure why, but I love orderly rows of planted orchards.

We make the turn to the Bruning farm. The popping sound of gravel under the tires startles the White Leghorns in the fenced-in yard beside us. Their heads bob up; they strut away a little alarmed but then get right back to pecking the ground. Nan greets Yvonne with a smile when she walks up to attend to us. They speak in French and despite Nan trying for years to help me understand the language, I hardly make out what they are saying.

I help lug the crates filled with cartons of eggs to the trunk of the car. Nan always tells me to be careful, even more so because I dropped one of the crates last year. What a disaster! Each time she does that, I remind her that I couldn't help it that a chicken got in my way. But each time she gives me one of her *silent looks* that pronounces that it was my fault or that a tiny little chicken is not responsible for my fallible human error. I decide that she and Grandmother must stay up late at night perfecting these silent looks that communicate more than words just to rattle me.

Upon our return, I walk into the kitchen with the screen door slamming behind me and my arms filled with groceries. The aroma of Nan's stew brings a smile to my face. It has been simmering on the stove all afternoon and welcomes us. After putting away all the groceries, I help Nan set the table for supper.

My mouth begins to water as I watch her ladle out portions of steaming stew. I cut the French bread and retrieve fresh butter from the fridge. A green salad, eaten after the stew, is set on the sideboard. Nan opens a bottle of Bordeaux and slowly pours the dark liquid into three glasses. *I can't wait until I'm old enough, so I don't have to have mine diluted.*

The front door remains open and through the screen a hint of spring wafts into the dining room. After we sit down and have our toast, Grandmother and Nan begin to talk about the plans for the big Easter Egg Hunt and other festival preparations. I don't join in much because I am savoring each bite of Nan's stew, which is a favorite of mine, along with dipping my French bread into the sauce. *Yum!*

Once I wash the dishes and put them away, I run upstairs, and head for my open window to feel the change in the air as the sun sets. There's a cool evening breeze we often get from the ocean air this time of year though we are miles from the coast. I like to pretend that the ocean is just a few blocks away when the air flows this way because it makes me feel as though we are on holiday.

Yes, the treetops are moving and there is a growing chill in the air. I put on a sweater and bound down the stars. As usual, I am the first one ready for our evening 'constitutional walk'. I rush to our front garden to be alone for a few moments.

The colors of all our flowers are brightest this time of evening. The Four O'clock and Evening Primrose have opened. Yellow and red daffodils stand tall and roses on the arbor shower down a cascade of pink and red with splashes of green. I close my eyes for a moment to inhale the sweet scent of lemon blossoms and honeysuckle, and then let out a sigh. The sun has just set, and the sky is periwinkle. It's magical.

I turn to the sound of the screen door whooshing open. Grandmother and Nan carefully walk down the steps arm in arm. She steadies her descent with Nan on her right side and her ladies' cane on her left. She only uses her cane on private occasions since she tripped on a raised root and fell on one of our walks last year. It seems that her swollen knee hasn't been the same since. Dr. Monroe insists that she use the cane anytime she walks, as Nan reminds her, but, in public, vanity is her chief advisor. She had to remain in bed for almost a week when it happened. I have noticed a change in her, as if the injury took something else away besides her dignity.

The three of us stand in silence soaking up the evening all dressed in its glory. After a few minutes, Grandmother speaks, "Shall we go?" One by one we walk through the magical arbor and out into the night.

Back home in my room, ready for bed, I grab my hymnal for the pageant. I wish I could play the notes on our piano, but everyone is already in bed for the night. I'll just have to suffice with my own solo. I read the lyrics of *A Morning Song for the First Day of Spring,* the hymn we are to sing for the invocation. Ever so softly, I begin singing:

> *"Morning has broken, like the first morning*
> *Blackbird has spoken, like the first bird*
> *Praise for the singing, praise for the morning*
> *Praise for the springing fresh from the word*
>
> *Sweet the rain's new fall, sunlit from heaven*
> *Like the first dewfall, on the first grass*
> *Praise for the sweetness of the wet garden*
> *Sprung in completeness where his feet pass*
>
> *Mine is the sunlight, mine is the morning*
> *Born of the one light, Eden saw play*
> *Praise with elation, praise every morning*
> *God's recreation of the new day"*[ii]

My voice, not as elegant as Elizabeth's who usually does the solos, still blends well with other voices around it. Yet here, alone in my room, as I gaze out of my window at the evening and the crescent moon, my voice feels pure and beautiful, as if I am singing to God himself and He is listening only to me.

The Kiss

I have to leave for school a bit early today to take the eggs to the cafeteria where we will do our egg decorating after school. After a few more fast twirls in my mirror, I go down to our kitchen where the colorful eggs are ready to take to the car.

"Not so fast, mon petit," Nan admonishes. "You must eat breakfast first."

"Well, can it be a fast breakfast? I need to take the Easter eggs to school."

Nan takes a bowl of fresh eggs out of the fridge. "It will take only a few minutes to whip up these eggs," she says.

I love to watch her cook, so I go and stand next to her. "Can I crack one?" I ask.

"Certainly! But be careful, I don't want the yolk to break."

I do just as Nan taught me. I crack the edge carefully on the rim, open the shell slowly and out drops the egg.

"Oh my gosh!" I exclaim. "Nan, look here! There are two yolks!"

Nan peers over, wipes her hands on her apron and states matter-of-factly, "Do you know what that means?"

"No. What?"

"In numerology two can mean many things: serving others, forgiving and not liking conflicts are a few of them."

"Really? How do you know this?" I wonder. "And how can you remember so much?"

Nan lifted one eyebrow, "Because, mon petit, I have a passion for the numbers! Now, I'll whip you up that double-yolk egg."

Nan scrambled the golden, buttery addition to my plate along with a slice of toast. As soon as I tasted the egg, I said, "I like this double-yolk egg. It's richer."

"Like you will be someday," she says.

"Rich?"

"Yes. That sounds good, doesn't it?" she said, turning to clear away items from the kitchen counter.

"I guess. I don't care now. Maybe when I'm older!" I quickly finish and put my plate in the sink.

"Just remember like the numbers tell us with that double-yolk, always try to *serve others*...so don't forget to rinse off your plate. You know how eggs stick," she said, with her funny-stern look, but then she smiled at me.

I did as I was told. "I have to go now! Oh, thank you for the twin yolks, and their meanings." I grip the handles of the egg crate firmly with both hands, lift it up, and then prop the bottom of the crate on my hips for extra support. After kicking open the screen door, I carefully maneuver down the steps one at a time, and then waddle like a penguin towards our car. I notice Jimmy opening his gate. I stop and yell, "Hey, Jimmy, wanna ride to school?"

He looks straight at me, then slightly cocks his head. Upon seeing my strained expression—he quickly and without answering—rushes over, stands in front of me, grips the handles and says, "Let *me* take that. *You* get the door."

I just smile sweetly while flapping my eyelids (mimicking Bette Davis) and do as he says.

Jimmy places the crate safely in the back seat, turns to me, and says, "You should not be trying to carry such a heavy crate. I guess I will *have* to get a ride with you so I can carry the eggs into the cafeteria. We don't want them to break!" He hesitates and then adds jauntily, "Besides, you might ruin your pretty yellow dress."

"Thank you, Jimmy," I say softly. I thought it strange that I didn't have any objection to his help; in fact, I was surprised at myself for secretly wanting it. I do like that he likes my dress. But it's funny—he's never seemed to notice what I wore before. *What's going on with him anyway? Gosh, what am I going to wear for the pageant tomorrow, maybe my blue dress?*

On the way to school, Jimmy and I sit in the back seat with the crate between us. We don't say much to each other, but Nan asks all kinds of questions about the decorating plans and such for the day that I supply her with answers, but a little brusquely.

When we finally get to school, Nan pulls around close to the cafeteria and cautions us again about not breaking the eggs. Jimmy's glance catches mine, and he smiles handsomely. *Oh, there are those goosebumps again—I think I'm beginning to like them.*

"Don't worry Nan," I say, quietly and sigh. "Jimmy will carry them."

I walk beside him while he lugs the crate (noticing that he carries the heavy crate with ease) to the cafeteria door and I open it for him. After we give the crate to Mrs. Lake, one of the cafeteria ladies, and we walk out, still not saying much to each other. Finally, I turn to Jimmy and tell him, "See you later to decorate."

At the same time, he says, "You know the spring dance?"

At the same moment he says *dance*, I say *decorate*. We both stop talking and stare at each other. Was he asking me to the dance? Did I hear him right?

"Sarah," Jimmy says, "Would you be my date to the spring dance in a few weeks?"

"Oh, my goodness!" I blurt out. I can feel my face getting hot and I just want to hide. Jimmy is kind enough not to say anything about the color rising on my cheeks and waits for my reply.

"Sure. That would be nice."

We both stand awkwardly. Jimmy says as he turns to go toward his class, "It's a date then. See you later to *decorate*."

I watch him walk away and wonder who he's been talking to. I never heard him speak to me like that before and I notice that my stomach feels strange. I wonder… with all those chills… am I getting sick? I hope not… Oh, what am I going to wear to the dance?

Throughout the day, I have difficulty concentrating on my schoolwork. What am I going to say to Jimmy later when it comes time to decorate those eggs?

On the way to the cafeteria, I spot Jimmy. He's talking with a group of his friends and doesn't seem to notice me. I hurry past them because I still don't know what to say to him, especially in front of his friends.

Inside, the supplies are all set up. Mrs. Lake hard-boiled the eggs during school and some of the mothers are also helping by preparing the dying solutions. Each table has seven small cups filled with perfect Easter colors; pale green, pink, bright yellow, lavender, blue and aqua. *How pretty!*

I sit next to Carol and Elizabeth, two of my classmates. Mrs. Lake walks by and reminds us to wipe our hands so our clothes won't stain. I pick up my first egg and carefully place it into the bright yellow liquid. As I'm gently turning the egg with my fingertips, I notice Jimmy walking right to our table. He's staring directly at me!

He grins when he sees my reaction to him, sits down to my right, picks up an egg from the basket and places it in the cup with the blue dye. I gather courage to look up at him and I see that his smile persists. Finally, I begin giggling and then we both burst out laughing and giggling at each other, smiling knowingly, then mysteriously, as if we shared the greatest secret the world had ever known.

After all the eggs are done and ready for the next day, we walk home. The April afternoon is breezy, and the wind keeps flipping my hair about. Strands end up in the corners of my mouth and I have to continually pull them out and brush them back behind my ears.

Jimmy tells me that he would have waited to ask me to the dance, but since he was going to be out of town all week, he didn't want anyone else to get a chance to.

I smile sidelong up at him.

We come to my house first and stop at the stairs. We are awkward, standing beside each other in silence. A gust of wind unravels my hair again. Before I get a chance to, Jimmy combs my stray hairs with his fingers and tuck them behind one ear. Shivers roll up my spine. Jimmy smiles, and as he begins to walk away, he says, "See you tomorrow."

"Bye," I say. I watch Jimmy as he walks away and notice that he has certainly changed. He's become tall, lanky, with broad shoulders and strides with long-legged confidence. When I turn, my face almost smashes into the rose bush! I look back to see if Jimmy had seen my awkwardness, but he didn't.

Walking slowly down the path and through the side gate, I start to ponder. I have always wanted someone to ask me to a dance, but I never thought Jimmy would ask me. Now, it feels like I don't even know him even though I've known him forever... What am I going to wear?

Thursday, April 14, 1938

The pageant is like a kind of county fair in miniature. There are different acts, skits, and parents yelling out commands like carnival barkers. Oscar, who sits next to me in Miss. Osborn's 5th grade English class is dressed like a giant Easter egg for one of these skits, poor guy. His head, legs and arms protrude out of the holes in his hard egg costume, which makes walking a challenge. While he is going up the steps to the stage to do his skit, he trips on the last one and begins rolling around helplessly, waving his arms and kicking his legs while we all laugh and carry on.

Someone is mean enough to call him 'Humpty Dumpty,' and soon the entire audience is chanting 'Humpty Dumpty sat on a wall. Humpty Dumpty had a great fall...' I start to feel sorry for him and then reconsider. *Aw, he probably did it on purpose. He is the class clown after all and he's probably reveling in it.*

I start to feel nervous because the last event that follows our attempt at theatre is the showcase of our vocal ability, our choral recital. I stand next to Elizabeth, who towers above me.

She's wearing a pretty dress that is all in green. Since she is a sixth grader, I wonder why Jimmy didn't ask her to the dance, but instead asked me. After all, she sits next to him in math and she's one of the most beautiful girls at school.

I look over at Jimmy and think about *my* dress. I think it's prettier than Elizabeth's. It's baby-blue eyelet with puffed short sleeves and has a full skating skirt that twirls wonderfully. Also, the white sash daintily tied around my waist emphasizes my budding figure.

I straighten out my skirt and stand as tall as I can. The choir director raises her baton and we begin. The cacophony of kids laughing and yelling, family members chatting and teachers repeating insistent "shushes" suddenly quells as our soft voices float up and out over the auditorium. I know that we never sounded this good in rehearsal and the effect is magical.

At the end of the 'Morning Song', we wait in the last beat of our breath for the applause. I glance over at Elizabeth and see that she has a look of bliss and is so sure of herself. Suddenly, the audience, as if one body, rises and their reaction is thrilling. The frenzied cheering and clapping seem like it will never end.

Afterwards, while most everyone enjoys the refreshments in the lobby, the fifth and sixth graders gather at the cafeteria to get their baskets of decorated eggs to hide. Some of them have notes attached announcing prizes for the finder. We have to conceal these cleverly, yet not make it too difficult for the younger kids to locate. Jimmy grabs his basket and follows me handsomely out to the yard.

Trees and bushes are the best hiding places. The older kids place some of the eggs in obvious spots for the younger ones since they get to go first and fill their baskets. After that, it's a free-for-all. I think the prizes are exciting to them as they were to me when I was little. Everyone saw them displayed in the office for two weeks now, and everyone has already "owned" the prize they are going for. Even though I'm a fifth grader, I wish I could participate this year. I so like the little train set.

The bell goes off for the students to begin finding the eggs. Everyone is smiling watching this tradition unfold. Quick successions of one kid after another yelling, "Here's one!" or "I found one!" and before we know it the hunt is finished in a flash. All that effort, I think, for a momentary thrill.

Jimmy and I catch up with his mother, Nan and my Grandmother back at the auditorium. They immediately give the whole pageant many accolades and share their amusement, as we did, about Oscar's comedic talent. I noticed that Oscar, a peeled egg now, is getting many pats on the back topped with smiles. I laugh thinking that he does make a perfect Humpty Dumpty being short and squatty; with any luck he'll grow out of it. Maybe he'll even have a future career in show business because he rather reminds me of Charlie Chaplin's "Little Tramp". *He's no Jimmy Stewart though.*

The principal awards all the prizes to the lucky winners and we say our adieus. Jimmy and I agree that we will visit with each other later, especially as he will be leaving for his big trip the following day. During the ride home all Nan and Grandmother talk about are the preparations for the upcoming festivities. Nan appears a bit frayed so I tell her not to worry, that I will help.

I'm sitting at the kitchen table, my legs scrunched up into a ball, frosting cupcakes for Easter Sunday while Nan is preparing dinner. I think about how this day seemed to slip away. It reminds me how water slips through the cracks between my fingers when I try to cup my hands to drink.

"What a beautiful pageant!" Nan says as she chops onions.

"Uh huh," I agree.

"Oh, how the singing makes me cry."

"Yeah."

"I thought your voice was…well, it was more...how you say...more full of the soul than Elizabeth's."

I swirl the frosting in little peaks and just think about the dance...and Jimmy. "Uh huh."

"And, Oscar, he was so funny!"

"Uh huh."

Nan stops stirring and asks somewhat alarmed, "Sarah! Are you all right?"

"What?"

"You've hardly said anything since we got back home today… this morning too for that matter. What is on your mind, mon petit?"

My goodness! I can't tell Nan or Grandmother about Jimmy asking me to the spring dance. I know that I will have to, but I feel strange and embarrassed. I wonder what they will think. I blurt out, "Did you know that Jimmy is going to Los Angeles during the holiday and that he is going to go to some big movie houses and that he is going to try and get me an autograph from Jimmy Stewart!"

"Is that what you are thinking about, *movie stars*? There are more important things in life than the movies. You'll find out soon enough," Nan says, somewhat slyly.

"I suppose so," I say, now just a bit downcast.

I finish frosting all of the cupcakes and sprinkle each one with colored sugar crystals. Then, I take them down to the basement to put them in the pie safe so that they can stay cool until Sunday.

While descending the steep stairs, I almost tripped. The pan wobbles in my hand and luckily, only one cupcake falls. I watch it topple down the stairs as if in slow motion and then roll away, disappearing between two steps. An eerie feeling goes through me, as if someone is underneath and has grabbed my ankle for a split second. *That's crazy!* I think.

When I'm safely at the bottom, I set the tray on a shelf. Now, I have to find the missing cupcake, and of course, it rolled under the stairs into the darkest region of the cellar. I recoil at the thought of going back there. For some reason this is the only place in our basement that I don't like. For as long as I can remember, that particular spot has always given me the creeps.

The cupcake is nestled between two old wooden boxes. I don't know how it got there—of all places. As fast as I can, I reach between the shadows, grab it, and then feel a web clinging to my hand. *I hate spider webs! I should have just left it for the mice.* I brush off my hand quickly and make certain no spiders came along for the ride.

Our basement is quite large. To the right of the stairs is the pie safe. Ours is tall and wide, probably due to Nan's constant cooking and preparing for Grandmother's many events! Opposite the stairs are more steps and a door that opens to the side yard where my swing hangs from a limb of the Blue Oak tree. Left of the stairs is the beginning of our extensive wine cellar.

I'm in charge of dusting off bottles, turning them and checking to see that the labels are in their proper position and not peeling off. I also have to check the cork for any signs for spoilage and alert Nan. I don't mind doing that though; I love to read all the labels and feel like they are now old friends.

Many of the bottles are from local wineries; many are from France, and several from other parts of Europe. I've even given them names. For the French wines, I use French names like Antoinette, Marcel, and Francis. The local wineries often give Grandmother several cases of their futures as they use the grapes from her vineyards. Those wines I name after interesting characters on Main Street; Bob—he has a barber shop; Gladys is Grandmother's hairdresser and Frankie owns the hardware store—one of my favorite places. They even have art supplies there!

Before naming the new wines, I have to rest the bottle in my hands and study their color. Then, I think about the flavor and choose a name—from a person I know—with a personality that reminds me of the wine. Sometimes, I even choose schoolmates or one of their parents! Afterwards, I neatly write the name on the shelf beside the wine. We have hundreds and hundreds of bottles, a whole community!

I open the pie safe door and then laugh. Nan's freshly baked pies already fill three big shelves! Several are apple, a few are rhubarb and then there are blackberry tarts and strawberry tarts. They look just like they would in the store window at Bergen's Bakery. I barely manage to make room for the cupcakes and determine that I may have to raid this pantry if she keeps baking at this pace! I bound up the stairs quickly, trying not to think about the spoiled cupcake, the spiders, or the dark space where it had settled.

During dinner, Grandmother and Nan talk about the pageant and the upcoming picnic. All I can think of is Jimmy being gone for a whole week. Since we spoke about the dance these strange feelings have been welling up inside me, yet I have no idea how to talk about them or what they even mean.

"You have hardly touched your food, Sarah," Grandmother says.

I slyly grin at her and say, "I've had quite enough, thank you."

She smiles because I am improving my etiquette, but Nan blurts out, "Nonsense!"

"Oh. I guess I licked too much frosting or something."

Nan turns to Grandmother and says, "No, she's been acting strange all day. Maybe all this activity is exhausting her." Nan turns to me. "You should get to bed early tonight, mon petit, after our walk."

I nod.

After dinner and before our constitutional, I decide to go out to the backyard hoping to see Jimmy. The evening is warm and comforting. I hunt for flower cuttings for a vase while at the same time spying into Jimmy's backyard in a subtle search for him. Perhaps, he's getting ready for his trip or maybe he's still having supper? I instantly dismiss the latter because we always seem to eat later than anyone. Nan says that this is a tradition from France and I still don't know why.

I peer over the short picket fence between our yards for the fifth time and I suddenly feel that someone is watching me from behind. I turn quickly.

"I was wondering if I would see you before I left," Jimmy says quietly.

I'm glad it's dark because I can feel the heat rise up on my face again. "When are you leaving?" I ask, almost whispering.

"Early in the morning...it takes nearly a full day to get to L.A. from here." Then, he grabs my hand and says, "I want to show you something." His hand is warm, yet I feel that shiver again.

I follow his lead away from the porch light to the middle of our backyard. It's dark now. I can see the outline of his face in profile as he lifts his arm dimly to the stars.

"See those three stars?"

"Yes," I answer.

"Those are part of the constellation called Orion. In Greek mythology, he's called The Hunter and those three stars represent his belt."

Looking up in awe, I reply, "Yes, I remember hearing about that somewhere."

"Sometimes, the constellations, Canis Major and Canis Minor are considered his dogs!" he states in his rasping whisper.

"Really? How do you know so much about the stars?" I ask.

"I have some books about them. In Sumerian mythology, they called him Anu, the sky-god and he lived in the highest heavenly regions. There are images of him in my books. Sometimes it shows him holding a sword and other times a club. He is also the destroyer of the wicked."

"I never heard that before!" I exclaim.

Jimmy gazes into my eyes. His face moves closer to me and he gives me a gentle kiss on my lips. The sensation leaves me faint. When he slowly pulls away, I open my eyes, my face burning hot and he speaks, "So when I'm down there and you're up here just go outside at night and find Orion's Belt. I'll do the same and think about you, Sarah.

Handing Over

B arbara placed the section she'd just finished on the coffee table, walked into the kitchen and said, "I heard the water running."

"Yes, just finishing the dishes. All done?"

"I am. Sounds like Sarah at least recalled some pleasant memories," she said.

"Well those memories came later to me as I was writing my book," I said while wiping my hands. "How about we go sit on the couch."

"Sure. Oh, I was wondering if you would let me take a few chapters home to read. I'd like to keep the flow of the book fresh in my mind. I'll be sure to return them, and to take notes too."

"That would be great'" I said, with gratitude. "I'll get them for you."

We then discussed what she'd just read, went over a few corrections and she gave me her notes along with some questions I would take a look at later.

"Since some of these chapters have less pages, I'm giving you the next five chapters."

As I handed her the next section, Barbara glanced through the pages in the folder and said, "That looks like a perfect number of them. Thank you."

I held her hand and said, "Please, if what I wrote is too difficult to read without me there, just wait until you come back. All right?"

"Not to worry. I'll be fine." She paused then added, "At least I hope so!"

The sound of rolling thunder interrupted our conversation. I looked out at dense black clouds approaching. "Looks like it is going to start raining pretty soon. You'd better go before it begins to pour," I suggested.

"You're right." Barbara put on her coat and lifted her satchel. "I'll take heed of your concerns about reading. But I'm sure I'll be fine."

"See you tomorrow. Same time?" I asked.

"Yes, that's what I'd planned for, "she replied.

I gave her a warm hug. "You have no idea how much I appreciate your help." Barbara smiled and then dashed out to her car.

I sat on the couch, happy, grateful and relieved, in a way, to have encountered this newfound friend.

I'd placed a fresh cup of coffee on a coaster and watched while the rain began to drip rivulets down my wide paneled window. I thought about the morning and considered that it had gone well. I'd been writing the story of my past life, of being Sarah for about five years. I felt the story needed to be told, however, I had no idea that when I'd started that writing that its details would drastically alter the course of my life and change so completely who and what I thought I actually was. The sudden onslaught of my own psychic abilities coming simultaneously to my writing convinced me I needed to include how recalling a past life affected me in my present life in many different and unexpected ways. I thought about all the gifts of knowledge such experiences yield.

I now had a greater understanding of evil, suppression, multiple personalities and abuse. And thankfully I have come to personally know their opposites: courage, love, faith, and hope.

The task of how to include all my recent psychic experiences and how they were directly related to what I had uncovered had been perplexing me for over a year. Along with this, the wisdom gained from facing the horrors made me realize my two completely different lives were strangely becoming one. Sure, I had two sets of parents, two different bodies and was raised in two different towns, during two separate times, but now, because I had remembered the past so irrevocably, they were separated only by the act of bodily death.

I had tried many different approaches and perspectives to analyze and align the threads of this now bigger picture at least four concrete times with pen on paper and over a hundred in my head. In fact, it was when I'd finished the whole of my past life story that I began to seriously ask myself, "What about this one? What about all the miraculous experiences that have come into my life only because I had faced the evils of my past?"

In addressing those evils, I regained not only what I had lost but gifts seemed magically bestowed upon me for my courage to face what I could not escape but had to confront during my previous life.

When I was at my wits end as to how to combine my two stories into one, I met Barbara. Her offering to help gave me the chance to realize my hopes. To complete the task. Through our conversations the present and past lives began to merge more clearly.

I heard the rain now flowing down the gutter, pouring fast, like a small creek. The wind whipped pattering drops against my window. As I focused on the droplets, I pondered my two lives. They were like separate drops of water on my window-pane, coming close, slipping into each other, becoming one.

After Barbara got into her car, the clouds that were patchy an hour prior were now darkly ominous and suddenly broke into a downpour. At least I live nearby, she thought, then took in a deep breath and exhaled. I hope it's not as bad as Kerry suggested it might be, she thought.

On her way home she had glanced down at her satchel—which sat on the passenger seat—several times wondering what the contents of Kerry's next section might be. God, I wonder what's going to happen to Sarah? she thought.

The rain poured hard as she pulled into the parking lot of her condo. At least it's covered, she thought. Luckily, I didn't forget my umbrella. I'd hate to get her manuscript wet.

It was just a few months earlier when she had signed the lease and felt fortunate. The property was built in 1972 and she learned that these units rarely go on the market.

Barbara's unit was on the seventh floor facing northeast of the ten-story building. She enjoyed the view of lush treetops and far away vistas of the Sierra Nevada Mountains. Today, after she'd put her satchel on the table and peered out, all she saw were gray clouds, mist and the heavy rain slapping away at her balcony.

Having dressed in pajamas and a robe, she prepared dinner, then ate at the island facing the sliding glass doors to the balcony. She'd look over at Kerry's several chapters on the counter every so often, trying not to imagine what would be written there. I have to keep an open mind, she thought.

She made tea after dining and placed her teacup on the side table by her comfy reading chair.

Nestled in, she placed the stack of chapters on her lap and began.

Behind the Double Doors

Someone explained to me that the doctors completed my series of treatments, although I wasn't sure at the time what they meant. I walked slowly compared to others, and usually with someone else helping me keep my balance. I wondered if my slow movements had something to do with those treatments. When I did attempt to walk unassisted, I fell down. Then I would lie there until someone helped me up. Each day passed quietly, like a dream. Mostly, I sat outside on a bench under the trees. When people asked me questions, having no desire to answer I hardly said anything to anybody.

I noticed that each morning the sun rose, I began to feel a little stronger. After some time, I was able to wash my face and to bathe with less help, except each night I had difficulty waking up to go to the bathroom. Most often, I would wake up to wet sheets. I didn't like going to the bathroom in bed. My legs were wet and smelled and the nurses yelled at me. I learned that there was always a time to eat, to sleep and do nothing. I learned too, that everything revolved around the hospital bells.

I had met this girl named Patty. She said we knew each other before my treatments, but I had forgotten because of them. She also said that someday I would remember. I'd remember everything and she'd help me. She was nice enough. I liked her.

Patty helped me not make a mess when I went to the bathroom. I sat up straight. She said it was very important to sit up straight. I did better and didn't splash. Every day she helped me learn how to take care of myself better.

Patty also took me to the cafeteria to eat and to the community room most afternoons to listen to the radio. I didn't mind going to the community room with her. She made me smile. She never missed her favorite radio show and never went without me.

"Sarah, come on. It's time," said Patty as she stood at the open door to my room. Patty's long brown hair, pinned up neatly, outlined her light skin and unusual crescent smile.

I was glad to see her. Then I realized I was glad and smiled.

"Come on, Sarah! It's going to start soon," she exclaimed and walked to my cot with her arms outreached.

I had been sitting there for a while just staring out the high windows at the blue sky. "O—kay—I didn't—know—it was time," I finally managed to say.

"Here, let me help you get up. When are you ever going to get back into the *sa...wing* of things?" Her words flowed with the movement of a swing. "Sarah, tell me, will ya? It's the 'Longine hour'. My favorite, our favorite I mean, radio show," she said. Patty practically lifted me off the floor with her excitement.

"O—o—okay," I replied.

Even with Patty's help, my legs still felt heavy and shuffled on the wood floors as we walked slowly, arm in arm, down the hall. Patty never ceased talking.

"My daddy sent me a letter this morning. He's doing much better with his business and he said that he knows I'm doing better too. In fact, he said that I really didn't need to be here any longer. Soon he is going to be able to get me and take me back to New York with him. Have you ever seen New York? I haven't. But he has sent me wonderful postcards. I'll get them out and show you. I hope he comes soon."

"There's Catlady's room. I wonder if she is in there." Patty asked as her head stealthily peered in ahead of us.

As we walked by, we both dared to glance in quickly, half expecting her to begin screaming at the air that very moment and half hoping not to see her or at least not have her notice us if she did begin to yell.

There she was sitting on her cot, not talking today or at least not as we were walking by. She looked at us though. I noticed for the first time her eyes appeared empty, and in my mind, I pictured a pond without a reflection.

With her hand cupped over the side of her mouth, shielding her words from Catlady, Patty said softly, "It must be our lucky day... the cats are out to play!" Then she hurried me by the door.

Lucky day? I don't feel lucky being here. These past few weeks I began remembering my past in little bits and pieces like Patty said I would. I remembered a little about Jimmy and wondered where he was and why I hadn't seen him. I remembered Nan, Grandmother and Roberto. *Where are they?* Tears began welling in my eyes. *What did I do wrong? Why don't they come and see me?*

Patty gave me a comforting smile and clasped my hand firmly as we continued our trek down the long empty hall until we finally reached the doors to the outside.

For some reason I felt nervous and angry. I didn't know why, but I didn't want to move so fast. Patty was rushing me to get to the community room. I yanked my arm away hard and blurted out with short breaths in between words, "I can— get there on my—own!"

Patty turned, surprised at my outburst and then her head tilted. "I'm sorry Sarah," she said gently, "forgive me."

I stood there with my hands fidgeting, turning in their palms, and trying to stop the anger. Then, all I could do was sob.

Patty put her arms around me, wiping the tears from the tip of my nose and cheeks with a little white kerchief that had roses embroidered on it.

"There, there now Sarah, I'm sorry. I didn't mean to rush you. Forgive me, won't you? I'll never forgive myself unless you forgive me first," she pleaded.

My body shook with quivers and uncontrollable sobbing. I couldn't talk, even though I wanted to tell Patty that it really had nothing to do with her, that I didn't know what was wrong. I just felt angry, sad and tied up like knots inside.

We sat down on a nearby bench under the shade of a big tree. Patty, with her arms wrapped around me, held me like a small child, rocked me back and forth, and spoke softly, "I know what you have been through, Sarah. I know that it hasn't been easy for you or for anyone here. There's a lot of sadness here." She gently patted my shoulder and continued, "I have seen what shock treatment can do to other people. My mother, she had some treatments and I remember afterwards that she would feel angry and very nervous. I've seen it in other people too. All you have to do is look around and see. Many other patients have even been through much worse. However, you Sarah, you are different. Somehow, I know that you will be okay. Believe me, I just know."

I glanced up at Patty, my tears beginning to dry, and managed a stilted smile.

"See. You're better already," she said. We sat quietly under the shade of the tree, with her rocking and holding me tight, until my sobs slowly dissipated. "Now, how about some nice music to lift our spirits?"

We got up and continued down the path to the community room. The building stood tall with big glass windows around it. In front was a statue that used to be a water fountain. When we walked in a few people stared at us. One was Bobby. He was in his wheelchair by one of the large windows that framed the courtyard in the back. He gave us a wide smile, but it was mostly for Patty. She walked up to him and gave him a big kiss on top of his forehead. He blushed.

Bobby was about Patty's age, around fifteen. He combed his hair neatly and was thin except for his large arms that pushed the wheels of his chair around. Patty said that he had been getting worse, that he had some kind of disease. She said that when he was little he could walk fine, but that whatever is wrong with him just gets worse and worse. She also said that in the last few months, his left side seemed to be getting weaker, and that was why he always had his head tilted to one side.

Even though Bobby was sick and even though he was in this awful place, he kept his spirits up. He would tell us jokes that I had trouble understanding because of his slurred words.

However, Patty always laughed. I wasn't sure if she understood him, but she always managed to laugh at what seemed to be the right time.

After we sat down and assumed our regular places on a bench next to Bobby, I gazed dully around the room. But I felt as though I were seeing it for the first time. I thought of San Francisco, reminded of it as if fog was lifting. Everything seemed to be a bit more in focus.

On the right of us was an enclosed counter and behind it on the walls were cupboards that had some glass doors. I could see medicine, supplies inside, and that locks were on the cabinets. To the left of the enclosed cupboard area were two big doors. For some reason, I couldn't take my eyes off the large doors.

"That's where they do it," she stated.

What is _it_? Even Bobby looked up to see. I thought that maybe I was supposed to know so I didn't say anything.

"That's where they cut into you." Patty added.

All three of us were staring silently at the two doors that now loomed over the room. Each door had little square windows, set up high that appeared like two dark and empty eyes—waiting. I wondered what was behind those doors. Were there secret rooms where these—these operations took place?

All at once, we turned our heads to the silhouette of a man in a dark suit entering the glass doors at the visitor's entrance across the room. He walked in quickly, stopped, took off his hat and glanced around the room until his eyes located the reception counter. As he continued in his hurried manner to the nurse behind the counter, an eerie feeling came over me. There was something hauntingly familiar about him. He appeared to be in his thirties, had a medium build, white skin, black hair, with no mustache. I wondered what was so important that he didn't have a mustache. *Is there someone I know that has a mustache?*

After speaking briefly with the reception nurse, our eyes followed him as he walked straight towards the ominous double doors!

"My, he's—a brave—man," I managed to whisper.

"No, Sarah," Patty whispered back, "I don't think he is a patient. Probably a relative of someone in here."

"Relative of whom?" I asked.

"Oh, I don't know. I've never seen him before."

"Hey, look," Bobby, slurred out. Our eyes darted towards the doors. When that man went through them, the right one stuck open. Before someone closed it, all three of us stretched our necks forward to steal a peek down the ominous hallway.

A doctor came up to the man in the dark suit. He seemed familiar too. He was short and stocky. His face reminded me of a bulldog with rounded folds on his cheeks and chin, except his skin was very white, an odd color really, as if he never walked in the sun or something. He didn't have any hair. No, he did have some hair. It was just on the sides though, above his ears. It was light, either gray or white, and stuck out as if it hadn't been combed.

They shook hands, smiled. The man in the dark suit was talking, but we couldn't hear. The doctor wore a serious face and glanced down at his clipboard. He nodded, shifted his gaze and stared straight at us. As if one creature, we all drew our heads back. The man in the dark suit turned and looked at us too, *or was he looking at me?* With that thought, a chill hit the back of my head and sent my body to tremble. The doctor shut the door. *I don't like him.*

"That, my friends, was the one and only Dr. Frizz-brain," Patty stated as she let out a sigh. Bobby stuck out his tongue.

"Bobby, you shouldn't, he might see you," I said, still trembling.

"Oh, Bobby has nothing to worry about, he's already slightly crippled," Patty said.

My eyes frowned at Patty chidingly. Her use of the word *crippled* seemed rude and unkind.

Surprised at my being reproachful, Patty assured me, "Bobby and I have already discussed this a lot. He's not offended, are you Bobby?"

With that, Bobby feigned a sniffling sob. We all began to laugh.

"But why do you call him Dr. Frizz-brain," I asked. "Is it because of his hair sticking out?"

Both Patty and Bobby let out a giggle. "No, silly, he is famous for shock treatments, better known as frizzing brains," Patty explained.

My eyes fell shut. Patty's words faded. She spoke but seemed far away. I felt as though I were falling into an abyss.

Patty turned to me and said, "I'm sorry Sarah, I didn't mean...." She softly touched my head, stroking my hair. "Please, forgive me."

Her touch brought me back. I managed a slight smile although my mood shifted back to empty sadness.

Patty pointed at the big white clock above the reception counter. "Hey, it's almost three o'clock. That means the music is about to start. Let's go ask the nurse to turn on our program."

She took hold of my hand and gently pulled me to my feet. With her arm in mine, we walked to the nurse seated on the other end of the counter.

Behind the counter was the radio. Patty complained that this radio didn't have the sound of the one she used to listen to at home. They had bought it from the Sears catalogue store just last Christmas, but at least it worked. When the nurse turned the radio on, Patty gave her "the Patty look", a tilted eyebrow and pout that meant the sound was much too low. The nurse shook her head and turned it up just a bit to please Patty. On our way back to sit by Bobby, Patty walked in step to the music.

I never heard that slow tune before. "What is that?" I asked Patty.

"Oh, I don't know," replied Patty. "Let's be sure to listen to the announcer when it's over."

I noticed that the nurse behind the counter was smiling and tapping her fingers to the beat. Even Bobby seemed happier as his head bobbed back and forth with the music. On the other side of the room was an old lady, short and dumpy in a cotton dress, who just sat, unmoving. I wondered if she even heard the music. Some other kids, younger than me, were fooling around, but their noise didn't bother me. They were on the far side of the room. On the bench against the wall to my left were two men with a chessboard between them. Patty and I had nicknamed them *Mutt and Jeff,* like the cartoon strip. They fit the names perfectly and even had big mustaches! They weren't moving. Actually, they never move. Patty, Bobby and I had bet on it for fun. Who would be the first to move? I chose the short, balding man on the left, *Jeff,* nearest to us. Patty and Bobby chose the other one who was tall and skinny, *Mutt.* The only rule was that it couldn't be a body function movement, like a sneeze or yawn, but they had to move a chessman. Even though we knew they would just stare at the chess pieces all day, watching them gave us something to do.

"A beautiful new song, titled *Embraceable You,* by George Gershwin. Now, *Begin the Beguine,* the smash hit of last summer. Still a favorite, composed by Cole Porter," intoned the announcer.

"*Embraceable You,*" sighed Patty. "Wow, what a wonderful title."

I thought the song was pretty, but at the same time made me feel homesick. I remembered Grandmother and longed to see her again, to be back in our home, and to be on my swing by the side door near the kitchen. I thought about Jimmy and Orion's Belt and wanted to cry again.

"Bang!" reverberated the large doors, echoing off the walls of the recreation room, abruptly clouding my reminiscence. The man who had gone down the mysterious hall now came barreling out. All three of us watched as he exited as fast as he came in. This time however, he seemed upset. When he was about to leave at the front entrance, he stopped suddenly, turned around and scanned everyone in the room. He made strange faces, first with anger and then pity, as though he had to leave us all behind. After firmly placing his hat on his head, he turned and walked out, as if never to return.

Bobby, Patty and I stared at each other, puzzled, and then glanced towards the yet open entrance to the hallway. Right inside the doorway, we saw an attendant push a gurney with somebody underneath covered in a brown blanket. He wheeled it out of the room that the man and the doctor were just in, down the hallway and out of sight.

"I don't think that person survived it," said Patty matter-of-factly.

She got up and went to the front window, on the side where the strange man had just left. I was too tired to get up and join her. So, I sat there, waiting for her to tell me what she saw. But I could see a long gray car pull slowly away, turn onto the tree-lined drive, and leave the hospital campus. Another car followed. After a few minutes, Patty returned to her seat. I noticed that her eyes were tearing up.

Bobby blurted out, "Well?"

She turned to us and began describing what she saw. "There was a gray car; the kind dead people were carried off in. The other man that had come in here before, you know the one with the hat that Dr. Frizz-Brain talked to, was standing and watching. I think it was his father." She paused a moment to catch her breath and then continued, "There was a big man in white clothes and a black belt. He pushed the same gurney that we saw in the hallway out to the car. The two of them—the driver and the big man—picked up the body." She bent over and whispered, "It was odd, when they picked up the body; it was like they were picking up a board."

Our eyes widened.

"Anyway," she said with emphasis, "that's when it happened."

"What?" we both asked.

"The blanket blew off."

Patty stopped talking. We waited. We knew that she would finish telling us when she was ready.

After a few moments, she spoke up again, this time more softly and hesitantly, "He was just a kid. He laid there—his tiny body pure white like angel's wings—nothing moved but his hair in the wind. I think I'd only seen him a couple of times, didn't even know his name." Patty wiped away her tears. "I should have made friends with him."

We both reached over to comfort Patty.

She continued, "The big man quickly grabbed the blanket, almost dropping the poor boy, before it blew away. I could see his father, yelling with his fist clenched. Then they put him in the back of the car and threw the blanket in, shut the doors, got in and drove off."

Bobby and I didn't speak. Patty didn't speak. I laid my head on Patty's shoulder, and she grabbed my hands. Then Patty placed Bobby's hand in hers. We all three sat, silently mourning the lost soul of our unknown friend.

I bowed my head and reached to clasp a medal around my neck to begin my prayer, but nothing was there. I wondered if I used to have one but couldn't remember. With my hand on my heart and in silence I began to pray, "God rest this young boy's soul. Please take him swiftly to Heaven where he won't remember this awful place." I prayed for his father, "May you find peace and comfort in your time of loss." As I thought about him and the last look, he gave us, it suddenly dawned on me that cradled in his concern was apathy. A frightful chill rushed down my spine as I wondered if our fate would also rest in the hands of Dr. Cox.

Patty held me closer. "Now, now you two. We'll be fine. I just know we will. He probably had some disease, maybe tuberculosis or something. Don't even think about what we were saying before. I was just making things up."

Even though I wanted to believe Patty, I had no real reason to. Nothing I've remembered, nothing I've seen or felt, has brought me hope that I would not receive the exact fate as that little boy.

Later that evening as I lay in bed, I thought about this place and its horrors and tears begged to be released. I don't want to be here. But I must have done something bad. I know that. That's why no one visits me. I dug my head into the hard pillow trying to go to sleep and escape this misery but no matter what, I couldn't.

The hours passed and my continuous crying made my eyes puffy and aching. Finally, I decided to pray. I got out of bed and knelt on the floor. With my palms together and my forehead resting down on the cot I began, "Please, God, help me. I know that I must have been bad. But I don't know what I did. Please, I've learned my lesson. Please, let me go home. I just want to go home." I tilted my head back and looked to the Heaven's so that God could see my pleading eyes.

When I turned to get back in bed, I noticed the three stars in a row, Orion's Belt. I thought of Jimmy and how he told me about Anu, the sky-god who lived in the highest heavenly regions. I wondered if I should pray to him too. After all, he was supposed to destroy the wicked.

"Dear Anu, I don't know if you know me, but we need your help. Could you please take your sword and rid this place of the wicked?"

After I crawled back onto my cot and slipped under the covers, I noticed that after my prayers, I felt a tiny bit better. I like the thought of Anu and imagined that he races down from the Heavens. He thrusts his gleaming sword out in front of him, piercing the darkness, and searches for evil in every corner of this hospital. Suddenly, out of all sorts of doors and windows, scamper the wicked doctors and nurses trying to escape like frightened mice. The brave Anu catches each one of them! Afterwards, we are finally free and left in peace. I sigh and smile feeling a spark of hope.

Exhausted from the day and now the night, I only wanted to sleep. Nevertheless, as I lay there, I kept thinking about my story of Anu. The more I imagined his success; a different feeling began to drape over me. It was soft and lovely, and the spark of hope grew into a gentle, flickering flame like a candle. Sweet memories and sounds drifted into my mind serenading me back home. Visions of my life before, of Grandmother, Nan and Jimmy, showered me with warm feelings.

I am standing by our piano, helping to turn pages for Annabelle, Grandmother. She is playing my favorite part from the Concerto in F minor by Chopin....

Holy Friday

The hammering trill of the woodpecker wakes me up early destroying my pleasant dream of beautiful piano music. Annoyed at the sound, I put on my robe which I lay on my feet during the night to keep them warm, over my white cotton eyelet nightgown. I slide my feet across the wood floor to the open window to shut it.

First, I scour the tree for the culprit making that racket and spot him on the very branch he's been pecking at since he arrived a week ago. The rapid-fire tapping has become a familiar cadence. Yet, the silence between his repeated knocks is just as annoying. After the woodpecker wakes me up, just as I'm about to fall back to sleep during his intermission, he begins his hammering all over again.

Jimmy said he'd be willing to shoot the woodpecker with his BB gun for me when I complained about the noise last week, but I gave him a 'don't you dare' look.

Jimmy! Oh, I'd almost forgotten. Jimmy is leaving today…Oh, no. He's leaving.

Gazing at the stars and holding his hand last night felt almost like a dream. I sigh, and then close my eyes to relive our first kiss again, a special moment I know I will never forget.

Hoping he hasn't left; I hurry down the staircase and rush to the living room side-window where I can see if their car is still in their driveway. It isn't. "Shoot," I say aloud. They must have left before dawn.

"Sarah is that you?" queries Nan from the kitchen.

"Shoot, shoot, shoot, I missed him. Now I won't see him for more than a week!" I'm muttering to myself, ignoring Nan in the background. I peek out the window one more time just to make sure he really is gone. Irritated, I answer, "Yes, Nan... be there in a moment."

Nan is making fresh coffee. I love its aroma but don't like the taste, unless of course it has tons of sugar and cream.

The back door is open, as are some of the front windows, which creates a cool spring breeze that wafts through the house. Nan's arm stretches over the stove in quick, proprietary movements, preparing eggs while the aroma of fresh berry muffins fills the kitchen.

"Did the smell of breakfast wake you?" Nan asks.

"No. It was that darn woodpecker again!"

"Yes, I just heard it, too."

"Jimmy left already," I mope.

"Oui, you told me they were leaving today. It's too bad they will miss the Holy Friday mass and the Easter picnic."

"It's called Good Friday here, Nan."

We've had this conversation every year for as long as I knew the difference. In France, they call it Holy Friday and she keeps telling me that she will always call it Holy Friday no matter where she lives.

Nan slowly shakes her head and looks down her nose at me making me conclude that she really must be practicing those silent looks with Grandmother.

"What time are we leaving for the service?" I ask.

"Since it will be at five, we will leave a little before four-thirty, I imagine. I want to arrive early so your grandmother does not have to walk as far. Her knee has been bothering her so much lately.

"Yes, I didn't want to say anything to her," I confess, "but I knew that it hurt her the night of the party. Do you think it will get better soon?"

"I certainly hope so. At least that's what Dr. Franklin has told her."

"What did Dr. Franklin say?" Grandmother asks as she enters the kitchen.

"Only that your knee will get better soon," I blurt out.

She falters just a second before correcting her stance. "Oh, it's nothing," says Grandmother, with a dismissive air as she brightly declares, "Nan, as usual, your breakfast smells delightful. Oh, the glorious berries and that hint of vanilla...fantastique!"

I rush to get her favorite coffee cup as she sits down carefully at the kitchen table. I fill the wide-mouthed cup with the sable liquid, place it with its saucer on the table and then gather the cream, sugar and spoon for her. I think of my dream and ask, "Why don't you play the piano anymore, Grandmother?"

"Thank you my dear," Grandmother says sweetly, as she lifts and pours from the porcelain creamer. "My hands have been aching and I really don't like missing so many notes."

I pout. "But you play beautifully even when you miss notes!"

"We'll see." She quickly glances at us both and announces, "Now, you know that today is a day of mourning, but Sunday always follows!"

"You say that every year, Grandmother!" I tease. She smiles elegantly at me, but I feel suddenly bereft of purpose and noiselessly wander back to my seat.

Nan raises her eyebrow and tells Grandmother, "Sarah is sad about Jimmy leaving for the week."

I spin around red in the face. "I am not!"

"You certainly did not appear very pleased this morning when you talked about it," disputes Nan.

"Well…we just have fun together," I say, a little sheepishly.

I'm beginning to get the feeling they know about the dance…and the kiss. I glare at both of them. They share a conspiratorially glance at each other, both incapable of disguising their knowing grins…as if they've caught my hand in the cookie jar and are currently holding back the evidence of their discovery just to wait for that precise moment to pounce…my glare shifts to pathos. I look beseechingly up at Nan, then at Grandmother. They find they can no longer contain their laughter.

I'm more disconcerted than ever. "What is it?" I cry out.

Nan, with tears in her eyes, controls her amusement first, "Well, well, ma chère…it 'tis no secret. Jimmy's mother told us that he had already asked you to the spring dance."

Grand, now I must fight the embarrassment. How not being a party to this little joke of theirs bothers me so!

"Yes," I finally say, rediscovering some shreds of my dignity, though my cheeks remain inflamed. "I was surprised, really. And anyway…it all happened so suddenly." I peer up at Nan and say somewhat breathlessly, "You did say he liked me, but I didn't believe you!"

Grandmother's tinkling laughter subsides. She sips daintily from her cup, then quietly comments, "Someday, Sarah, you will understand that grownups have been through most of the things you are currently experiencing. Believe me, dear, we know more than you think."

"I suppose that is so, "I respond, with a slight pout.

"What are you planning to wear to the dance, young lady?" Grandmother asks, changing the subject somewhat. At least this diversion calls to mind pretty fabrics and the latest styles.

However, I am still so nonplussed from their humor at my expense that I cannot think of a single proper potential couture.

I sigh. "I really don't know. I've thought about it a lot, but most of my pretty dresses are getting either too small or are no longer in fashion."

Nan speaks up, "I could alter something for you."

By both of our rolled glances, Grandmother and I dismiss this plan with an inference of 'not for the first dance!'

Grandmother pats my hand. "We'll go shopping next week. Since you are on holiday, how would you like it if we both take the train to San Francisco? We could go to O'Connor, Moffat & Co. and see the latest fashions from Macy's in New York and then visit some of our other favorite shops."

"I don't want anything too fancy, Grandmother."

"It's your first dance, Sarah," Nan protests.

"Yes. But I don't want to have the fanciest dress at the dance. That would be embarrassing and not very nice to the other girls," I say, mostly because I don't want to find myself standing out.

"Do not worry," Nan assures me, with her thick inflection. "Grandmother will help you find the perfect dress—not so dressy and not so simple."

I smile across at them. Despite the earlier bout of embarrassment, excitement begins to well up inside me. I feel so much better now that I have allies about the dance.

"Can we go to Sabella's at Fisherman's Wharf?" I ask.

"Of course," Grandmother says. "It's too bad that they haven't finished remodeling the Cliff House... I would have loved to have taken you there."

"When do you think they will finish it?" I ask.

"Those things always take longer than expected. Maybe later this year I suspect," she suddenly had a wistful look in her eye. "It was a favorite place of your grandfather's and mine."

"I can't wait to go." I began daydreaming about our trip and having fun trying on dresses.

"We'll have to embark early if we are to get everything you'll need."

Clearly, Grandmother thinks as I do. That we will require the whole day for shopping! But I am thinking only of myself. Poor Grandmamma. What about her sore knee? How will she manage to walk through all those shops and down those busy streets?

As Nan places our breakfast muffins on the table, she says with concern, "Per'aps Monsieur Frank should drive you. Walking on all those hills may be difficult since you hurt your knee."

"I will be fine, Nan," she replies stalwartly, and moves to stand up.

"Grandmother, I'd rather have Mr. Frank drive us. That way we can go wherever we want without having to get a taxi."

"I suppose you're right. Though riding the train is so romantic, don't you think?" But then she glances at the crook of her cane looped over the arm of the chair. She winces inaudibly from the pinch in her leg as she stands and corrects her stance. Then, concedes with a sigh, "Mr. Frank it is then."

After breakfast, I step out on the front porch. Even though I know that Jimmy has already left, I still hope to find him. *Maybe he stayed behind.* Silly Sarah, I say to myself. Leaning on the railing, I stare at his house and then his bedroom window. Someone had shut them. Their house appears vacant and feels empty. I feel empty. I sit down on the porch swing and cars pass by. Maybe, the McAllister's forgot something and will have to come back.

I have to prepare for Good Friday service and decide that I should take my bath. I reach for the screen door handle and see a tiny, folded piece of paper thumb-tacked to the façade of the door. My eyes widen. It says, 'For Sarah'

Gosh, I'm so nervous. Little thrills of joy sweep through me as I unfold the crackling paper. I feel like a princess and Jimmy is my dream come true, but what if….

Dear Sarah,

I wanted to see you before we left, but you weren't up yet. I'll try to get that autograph for you!

Happy Easter! Jimmy

I fold the paper back in half again and carefully put it in my robe pocket. When I get upstairs, I take out my diary and write:

April 15, 1938

I got a nice note from Jimmy today. I miss him.

I place Jimmy's message in my diary and tuck the leather-bound diary safely away.

Three pews back, on the left side of the altar, I sit next to Grandmother and Nan on the well-worn wooden bench waiting pensively for Good Friday Mass to begin. I realize, as I attempt to swing my feet while I'm waiting, that they now touch the ground. Instead of a swishy soft sound from free-floating patent leathers, I hear a scratchy scraping sound, which alerts Grandmother that I am being inattentive. I stop.

I glance around at the pews filling up. No one else sits here. This is our pew. We have been in the same respective seats for the mass since I can remember— except on those occasions when we attend weddings and the attendants escort us to the right side or to a different row on the left. Oh, and funerals. They are entirely unique to our relationship with the family. But, for all regular masses, this is where we sit.

The Church bells ring out from the tall steeple beckoning parishioners to enter. As more arrive, I note the richly embroidered red and gold fabrics on the altar, though I find the black swatch in the center disturbing. One by one, the choir singers ascend the stairway to the gallery tower in anticipation of the mass, which reminds me of their ethereal voices raining down from above. The thought gives me chills except I know that today there will be no singing from them as they portray characters from the events of Good Friday.

I quickly turned to my favorite statue of the Blessed Virgin. Normally it appears as if her body were somehow frozen in time, though her soul is ever-present, warm and filled with the love of God. I like to think of her as an old friend that knows only the good in me no matter what I do. The azure color of her drape adds to her pristine beauty, but today they draped her in black cloth.

Latin service. The young deacon intones the words of the litany, when they took Jesus before Pontius Pilate and made him face the angry, murderous mobs of people. We are all enacting St. Luke's report of the events leading to Christ's death. Pilate argues that this man has done nothing. Then, as the deacon carries the cross to the altar down the center of the church, voices in the congregation began shouting harsh commands to "Crucify him!" For some reason the continuous catcalls fill me with panic, and I feel that I must get out of the church. I imagine escaping, but when I see the usher standing at the entrance, I know he would stop me. I picture him yelling at me, "Don't you know that Good Friday is a high holy day and that by your actions you will disrupt the sacred procession?"

I turn away from the usher and stare at the cloaked images and the bent back of the young deacon. The cacophony of voices echoes throughout the church and fills me with an overwhelming sense of terror. "I can't get out!" I scream inside. I feel squeezed and hemmed in, as if in my own coffin. I want to cry out, but I can't. I can't speak, though I try, I try....

I find myself staring up at the arches of the church. Grandmother bends over me, as does Nan, whose worry ministers a soft handkerchief of cool water to my brow. Grandmother has undone the first buttons along the throat of my dress. Two other parishioners have offered to help lift me from the floor, both older men that stand like two imposing towers above Grandmother and Nan. Trying to make sense of all these people perched around me makes my head hurt. I have to shut my eyes. Yet, even that makes me dizzy.

Grandmother insists that they place me carefully in the car. My head rests on Nan's lap in the back seat. I hear muttering sounds of parishioners through the open windows clamoring around car. Grandmother slides into the passenger seat in front of us. As we speed off, fresh air floods the car.

We take a long drive, while Nan lullabies me soothingly.

"What happened to me?"

"You fainted, dear. Perhaps it was too stuffy in there...so many people," says Nan.

"You'll be fine after breathing some fresh air," says Grandmother, with calm assurance.

"Try to relax."

I still feel shaky as we walk up the steps to our house. It's as if I have no bones in my legs. Nan warms some soup and insists I eat the whole bowlful. The soup helps, but for some reason I'm very tired.

Later, Nan helps me into my nightgown and then to bed. She comes back to my room in short order to make sure I'm tucked in and that I have a glass of warm milk and a slice of fresh bread and butter on my nightstand.

"Rest, mon chère. Take a little food. You will be well in the morning."

"So much for Good Friday," I mutter unsteadily. "I do hope that...that I didn't spoil the mass for you?"

"Well, at first I thought you were acting out a part in the Mass, but then...."

I interrupt her teasing, "Very funny, Nan—I can see the litany now...'girl faints as Pilate washes his hands of the whole situation'. Almost sounds like a news headline."

Nan places her large, warm and comforting hand on my forehead and closes her eyes, "Now be quiet for me." She bends forward hovering so close that for a moment I share her breath. In seconds, she smiles at me and says frankly, "Bon. No fever." Nan pats both of my cheeks softly, and then kiss each cheek grinning all the while. Her familiar reassurance comforts me, and I giggle softly at the tickling of her touch.

"What do you think happened?" I ask, pushing her away slightly.

She responds by adjusting my sheet with her deft fingertips. "Nothing to worry about my dear," she tells me. "Tomorrow, you will feel just fine. Besides, we will be too busy to concern ourselves. Now, go to sleep," she half whispers, sweetly. There's that dear old grin again. She studies my eyes just briefly, bends down and pecks my forehead and as she steps through the threshold of my door repeats, "Go to sleep, now. All is well."

I wonder why I felt so dizzy. I think of Nan comforting me and feel sad, like I want to cry. I don't know why. But I do.

In the middle of the night, I awaken to a softness issuing from my open window. It is not cold, only slightly sweet and breezy. I go to my window seat, kneel on the soft cushion and peer up at the stars. The indigo sky flickers with countless lights. I take in a slow, deep breath.

I feel so much better now, I think. How silly I was.

I wonder what Jimmy would have done if he were there? I imagine him holding me in his arms and I look up and gaze into his eyes. He kisses me on the forehead to comfort me.

Suddenly, I see a falling star with a long tail just above Jimmy's house. Maybe Jimmy is looking up at the stars at the same time I am. I think about Anu, the sky god holding his sword high into the air, destroying the wicked. I then look for the three stars of Orion's Belt. Just to the left they stand like three sentries guarding the heavens. As I scan across the sky for other shooting stars, I realize my eyes have become too heavy to keep me awake any longer. I best get in bed before I fall asleep on my window seat! After all, tomorrow is a big day. I have to help Nan prepare for Easter Sunday.

Catlady and the Rat

Three weeks had wandered by since that man came to the hospital and Patty told us about the dead boy's body. Bobby and I never brought it up again. We knew not to. Besides that, it was easier to forget the bad things if we didn't bring them up.

Today I felt brave. I don't really know why, I just felt different. Nothing had changed in my routine. I got up to the bells' loud clanging and took some pills that usually made me feel like I was wearing my dreams wrapped around my head like a mask, whether remembered or not from the night before. I cleaned and dressed myself. I was getting better at the routine, Patty even told me so. She had to help me less and less each day. In addition, today I felt that the mask of dreams had lifted. My thoughts seemed unchained.

All during breakfast, I was anxious to go outside, to remove myself from the loud din of the cafeteria and the taste of what they called food. For some reason Patty wasn't around yet, and I decided to venture outside by myself.

The courtyard appeared peaceful. Trees greeted me with warm colors and the air breathed the crispness of fall. I scanned the grounds hoping to find Patty under one of our favorite trees. I didn't see her but observed a strange old man sort of dancing off by himself and talking aloud. I couldn't hear his voice. How curious, I thought.

I heard Katherine's shrill voice and turned. She was in the middle of our courtyard by the east wall, her head bent backwards towards the sky or leaves, talking. No one ever spoke to her, I mean *ever*. Even the nurses just herded her as dogs herd sheep. Either they were afraid or maybe it was that she never spoke to them. They would just go up to her, and usually without talking, take her by the arm and guide her back to her room when it was time to go inside. Otherwise, I don't think she would know when to go in.

An idea entered my head. Without a second thought, I got up and walked right over to Katherine. She must be very lonely. She probably needs someone to talk to besides the air.

Katherine had her back to me. Her arms would go up each time she shouted a new sentence. Each time her arms raised my courage slipped a notch. Katherine wasn't a big woman, but there was this gigantic rage always present in her voice. It was such a strong energy that you could feel it, thick in the air. It also didn't help that I noticed weird winces on some of the other patient's faces. I mean, no one ever went too near Katherine, even by accident, and here I was walking straight towards her!

There was a tiny woman, another patient, who was sitting on a bench under a tree. I only knew her as being timid and sweet. She put her fingertips up to her parted mouth as I walked past her. Her eyes expressed a kind of shock I would rather not have seen. Two other women sitting next to her whispered to each other while both sets of eyes watched my every step.

I began to wonder, "What in the world am I doing? Everyone is staring at me." But for some strange reason, my legs kept right on walking slowly towards her.

I was now within a few yards of my destination. I could see Katherine's white scalp through the few wisps of brown hair left on her head. She wore a loose-fitting green gown and I noticed that her fingers on both hands never stopped twiddling, as if she would soon tangle them up into knots. She had a round, puffy face, indented with deep wrinkles. My legs stopped as I stood just two feet from her side.

Now, I wonder what I should do. I can't turn back or even turn around. All those eyes I passed are still warm on my back.

"Uh, hello?" I asked.

Katherine's reclining head remained so. She shouted to the air, "Now see that you do! If grandpa catches you in here…!"

The sharp anger in her words snatched my bravery. I began to turn around when I noticed the timid lady hiding her head under her arm and the two whispering ones had their hands half covering their eyes. For some reason the sight of these three women on the bench reminded me of the three monkeys, one covering its eyes, one its ears and one its mouth. So much so, I let out a chuckle. With a feeling of renewed bravery, I heard myself say to Katherine, "Excuse me."

Then even louder, "Excuse me!"

Slowly, her head lowered and without a pause, it turned a direct glare that cut right into me. I couldn't move. Up went her arms. "You! You!" She shouted and pointed at me. "You are an evil little girl, no one, no one likes evil girls. Back to the basement!" she shouted as she fully extended her arm with that unbridled anger and pointed towards the ground. Her head flung back to face the sky and she screamed loudly, "No-o one!"

I'd seen enough. I'd felt enough. I did so want to help her, but my bravery completely ran out. Suddenly, I found myself across the yard hiding behind a tree wondering if that was really me that had attempted to do what no one else dared. Peering around to view the scene I had just fled; I saw her arms lowered and fingers fidgeting. Her eyes appeared to weep. Moments later, she was back yelling again, "Stay in this basement and don't you dare come out!"

I waited until the commotion I created had quieted down. The three women quit seeking me out for my reaction. Katherine wandered farther away. I widened the distance between us even further by finding a big shade tree clear on the other side of the yard to sit under. But no matter where I went, I could still feel that jumbled energy and it scared me. I thought about what I had done, if it was right. I felt guilty, like I had upset Katherine, like I had stepped over my bounds.

Then I thought about how she cried one moment and screamed the next. It was like she was two people, one sad and one mad.

Later that afternoon I was in my room trying to forget my stupid bravery when Patty came by.

"You ready Sarah?" she asked.

I didn't answer.

Patty came to my bed, where I lay staring out the window, and she sat on the edge.

"Sarah, you wanna go now and listen to the radio?"

I didn't answer.

"What is it, Sarah? What's happened?"

"I—I talked—I mean I went right up and talked to Katherine, no, uh, Catlady, this morning."

"You did what?"

"I did…well…I don't know why, I just did."

"What in the world happened?"

"I—don't even want to talk about it," I replied.

Patty got that cute crescent smile on her face and said coyly, "I'll let you in on a secret."

"What?"

"I spoke to Catlady once," she whispered. "No, I did really. Believe you me. She looked right at me! Did she look at you? If she did that's enough to scare a fly from a horse's eye."

I began to laugh.

"She did, didn't she? I knew it. I could tell by the way you were acting. Did she say anything to you?"

"No, of course not," I answered softly, then added loudly, "but she yelled right at me!"

Now, we both began to laugh. The more we heard each other laugh, the funnier it seemed.

"Tell you what. I know just how you feel. What we'll do is sneak right past Catlady's room, so she won't see you. That way we can go and listen to the music, and besides, Bobby is expecting us."

I realized right there that I couldn't turn down Patty's requests. She made everything seem, well, not what I was feeling and almost like a fun game.

We began sneaking, tiptoeing, along with muffled giggles, all down the hallway. We noticed two women staring, cautiously pointing their fingers at me.

"You're their hero," Patty stated.

"No. No, I'm not."

"Oh, yes you are. Don't forget I talked to Catlady once and I became sort of a hero. You are the only other person that has been brave enough to talk to her beside me."

Even if Patty was wrong, she made me feel better.

Right before we were to pass Catlady's room on the left, to our right a woman jumped out from her door. "Ahhhhh!" we both screamed.

"I got it, I got it!" she yelled. It was Ratlady.

Before we could even ask her what she was talking about, she pulled this enormous rat out of her pocket by the tail! The biggest rat I had ever seen in my life! Then, she held it up, wiggling inches away from our faces!

It shimmied about between her upraised fingertips like it was going to jump out at us at that very moment! Both Patty and I screamed again and ran down the hall and out the door screeching and laughing. Not until we were well outside, did we realize that we had dashed right past Catlady's room. We were laughing so hard we fell down onto the soft green grass. It felt good to laugh in the sunshine.

Visitor's Day

Today was Saturday. Mostly, I didn't pay any attention to what day of the week it was, but for the past few weeks Patty and I, on this day, enjoyed going to the community room to watch the new people. Saturday is visitor's day.

Patty and I knew that we wouldn't have visitors. Her father couldn't come because he was in New York with his family, although she would get a letter from him almost every week. No one visited me and I never saw Bobby have a visitor either. Patty told me she knew he had a mother because she saw her a few times but that was before I came.

While we gazed at the other patient's relatives and friends wandering in, Patty piped up and said, "Oh, by the way, I got a postcard from my dad." She pulled a card out of the bag she always carried and handed it to Bobby. "It's from the World's Fair in New York. He said that he hopes to show it to me very soon and that a letter will follow."

Bobby and I stared at the postcard like it were candy. On it was a picture of the 'Trylon' and 'Perisphere'. It looked like a big ball and hairpin sticking up high in the air. It was a night picture with the sky full of fireworks.

Patty's face changed from dreaming to a cute quirky smile that I have come to know.

"You have that impish grin again," I said.

"It's a surprise, really," she quickly responded.

"What's it about?"

Patty pulled a brochure out of her bag. "Look at this!" She held it up for both of us to see.

"It's from the World's Fair at Treasure Island! It's the Official Guidebook."

"How wonderful," I said. "How did you ever get this?"

"My friend, Katie, sent this to me. She went there with her family for her birthday. Did you know that there is a 400-foot-tall building called the Tower of the Sun?"

"Really?" I said.

Patty pointed out the photo of the tower. It was a nighttime photograph and the tall tower was completely lit up. "I'd love to go there," she put her hand on her chin and sighed. "Can't you just imagine seeing the big statues a hundred feet high or the art? There's about, oh, I don't remember exactly, but millions of dollars of art—something like thirty or forty million. Half of it is from Italy. Can you imagine?" Patty paused, then said, "Okay. I want you two to close your eyes while I read you something. You have to imagine that you are there. Okay?"

"Otay," said Bobby.

We both closed our eyes and Patty began. She read it as if she was a stage actress; with each new word, she was painting a picture just for us.

"Great 70-foot-high walls of stucco, flecked with iridescent vermiculite (flakes of super-heated mica), have large circles of colored light to form contrasts against the ivory background, and floodlighted trees cast spidery silhouettes. Hidden in troughs, tucked in branches, clustered in tree baskets, almost buried under shrubs, are 10,000 colored floodlights, including 2400 pink, blue, gold, and green gas-filled fluorescent tubes, 130 searchlights and 300 ultra-violet mercury or "black light" lamps to produce the startling effect of color masses and patterns. Light is graded in intensity from the base of buildings to the top to maintain the depths of arcades and accentuate architectural setbacks."

I interrupted, "What's a black light do? How can light be black?"

"Yaaah," added Bobby.

"You two are so impatient. The next paragraph will tell you what it does."

"'Black light' projected on invisible weather-resistant luminescent paints in niches, on murals, and sculptures, produces the startling "colored pictures" that stand out in an almost phosphorescent glow against adjacent colored walls."

"So, the black light makes the special paint glow?"

"Yes, isn't that great?"

"Primary colors are mixed together to obtain new colors. Pink fluorescent tubes crossed by blue floodlights produce mauve. Trees lighted green stand out against the background of pale tinted walls. Fountains are lighted with their own colors. In the Court of Pacifica, a thyratrone behind the scintillating Persian Prayer Curtain produces a rotation of colors varying from dark blue to pale apricot.

"Switches and buttons on an electrical control board in each building are set permanently wherever the color scheme is static. Fountain lights are controlled from the bases of nearby statues. Controlling all these is a set of four switches on a master switchboard, which can be turned on at any given hour."

"I love colors. That sounds so beautiful! And complicated," I said.

Patty and Bobby both nodded.

"Overhead is a scintillator of light…"

I interrupted again, "I'm sorry, what's a scintillator?"

"It's like a crystal that makes sparkles or twinkles. I'll start that paragraph again."

"Overhead is a scintillator of light covering Treasure Island just a few feet above the 400-foot Tower of the Sun. Twenty-four gigantic searchlights, 36 inches wide, in eight different colors, are mounted on the north side of Yerba Buena Island. These army-sized lights, when turned on for special occasions, are manned by a crew of 24 and generate 1,440,000,000 candlepower of light visible for 100 miles."

Patty stopped reading and began flipping pages. "Why did you stop?" I asked.

"Oh, there's one more thing I thought you would like." She stopped her finger on a page and instructed, "Now, go ahead. Close your eyes again."

"The island's colors, stimulating, unforgettable, represent the first extensive application of chromotherapy—the science of health treatment by color usage. In the daytime, the effects are gained with flowers and tinted walls, at night, with fluorescent tubes, with the new 'black light', with ultra-violet floodlights, underwater lamps, translucent glass fabric pillars, and cylindrical lanterns 75 feet high. Some of the flowerbeds are played upon by artificial moonlight, others bathed in sunshine created out of neon and mercury. The $1,000,000 illumination program presents at nightfall the illusion of a magic city of light, floating on the waters of San Francisco Bay."

Patty stopped reading. "I know that I would prefer that kind of health treatment!" We all immediately looked at the ominous doors.

"Much better use of electricity!" I said.

The three of us made a fist. Patty put hers in first, I put mine on top of hers and then Bobby put his on the very top. We smiled and begged her to tell us more.

"I know," Patty said to me, "that you love the trees. So here's one more part I want to read to you."

"Meanwhile botanists were hunting through all the continents for unusual trees and plants. For many months' orchids, hibiscus, Datura, rare silver trees, orange trees, and palms were acclimated in a San Francisco plant hospital, where also are the electrically heated propagation beds that bring to bloom the plants to compose the ever-changing floral patterns of the fairgrounds. Horticultural plans call for planting 4,000 trees, 70,000 shrubs, and 700,000 flowering plants. To sprinkle the plants—and quench the thirst of visitors—San Francisco water was piped over the San Francisco, Oakland Bay Bridge to a 3,000,000-gallon reservoir cut in the solid rock of Yerba Buena Island."

"Just a minute, Patty," I broke in. "What is Datura? Did I say that right?"

"Just so happens I know! My grandmother actually grew them. It is a beautiful plant with trumpet shaped flowers. She had purple ones. You know what she told me?"

"What?"

"It is one of the 'witches' weeds,'" she whispered to us.

"Was she a witch? Your grandmother, I mean?" I asked.

"No. But she had a very large library and studied many different things, even Spiritualism! I used to love to visit her and read the titles on all the books." She hesitated then added, "I wish we had some of that plant here."

"Why?"

"Well, my grandmother always told me to be careful with Datura and not to eat it. She said that it could be deadly, or it could cause people to become delirious," she stated, recalling.

"So why was it called a 'witchweed'?" I asked.

"'Witches' weed'," she corrected me. "You see," she began, whispering again, "it is also used in love potions and witches' brews."

"How exciting! I wonder if it works."

A loud booming voice distracted our attention on flowery witchcraft. We all looked up to see who it was. In walked 'Tuba-man', Patty's name for him, of course. He was older, had a big belly and always brought in a stack of comic books tied up in string for the young man he regularly visited. The reason she called him that was because of his big stomach, his loud, low gruff voice, fat cheeks and because he ran out of air quickly. He never stayed long, only about ten minutes.

Following in behind him was a woman I hadn't seen before. She seemed the very opposite of 'Tuba-man'. For one thing, she was quiet, at least seventy years old and had a delicate build. She wore a light blue flowered dress and a white and blue hat. The reception nurse pointed past us in the direction of the back courtyard.

The bench where we sat was next to a half wall with the upper half all windows. Behind the wall was an enclosed patio next to the courtyard. All across the wall were floor to ceiling windows and glass-paned doors that led to the outside.

I got on my knees to see who the nurse was pointing to.

Just outside was that old man I had been noticing lately, the one that did a slow and strange kind of dance. The lady stood near us for a few minutes and just peered at him through the windows. In a moment, she turned her head, clutched her small white purse tightly, took a deep breath, and went outside. He didn't seem to notice her coming or pay any attention when she spoke to him. He had been talking to himself with his head lifted to the sky and continued to do so when she arrived. With his arms raised slightly upward, he made funny gestures with his fingers. He laughed, smiled and then presented a serious air. For some reason I was curious about them.

"Who is she?" I asked Patty, pointing to the woman.

Patty looked at me vaguely and said, "Oh, I don't know, probably his wife or maybe his sister, but they don't look alike. I'd say it was his wife more than likely."

"He appears as though he's in a play or something. Maybe he was a stage actor," I suggested.

Patty turned again and studied his movements. He didn't even notice the woman and continued with his antics. "I don't think he was an actor," Patty concluded. "He's been here since I arrived. But I don't pay him much mind. I think he looks a bit odd, though."

The woman sat on a bench near him. Yes, odd, I thought, he didn't even pay attention to her.

Then, I could tell he was ignoring her on purpose because at one point, she looked elsewhere, and he glanced down at her and smiled. Then, as soon as she turned back to him, he—in a very dramatic way—looked up to the sky with his arms uplifted as if he were talking to God. "That's strange. I wonder...," I began to say when the nurse interrupted me.

"Sarah, you have a visitor."

I turned, Patty turned, and Bobby looked up. The sun now reflected such a bright glare through the front windows that it was difficult for me to make out who it was, but even so my stomach felt uneasy with apprehension. I was in shock. As the figure walked closer, I could see it was a man. Patty grabbed my hand. He was average in size with dark hair and wore a dark suit. I thought he was the father whose young son had died. However, I could tell that he walked differently. The closer he came time seemed to wind down like a neglected grandfather's clock and each step towards me took longer and longer. All other sights and sounds faded away except for the shadow of a face hidden beneath his hat, and the pointed clap of his heels hitting the hard floor, which echoed above the din and beat the floor more loudly the nearer he drew.

He stood before me, removing his hat revealing a familiar, yet unknown face. His skin was fair, and he wore a mustache, but when he smiled, I noticed something about his eyes, something that frightened me. Quickly, I cast my eyes down.

"How are you Sarah?" he asked sincerely. I curled my knees up close to my chest and said nothing. "Why, Sarah, you remember me, don't you? It's your uncle, Uncle Joseph." I refused to look up at him. He knelt down, put his hand on my chin, prying it up until our eyes met. "You look quite well, Sarah. I'm glad. I've been so worried about you. I didn't come sooner because the doctor told me that you were not to have any visitors until now. You understand, don't you?" he asked dismissively, stroking the top of my head. He glanced at Patty motioning her to move. She let go of my hand and he then took a place between us on the bench.

I didn't like him. I didn't like the way he talked. I didn't want him touching my head and I didn't want to have an Uncle Joseph.

"Tell me Sarah, who are your two friends here?" he asked, smiling in a too familiar way, I felt, at Patty.

However, Patty, unlike me, was not afraid to speak up. "My name is Patty," she said proudly, "and this is our friend Bobby."

Uncle Joseph grabbed Patty's hand. "It's so nice to meet you. I'm certainly pleased that Sarah, here, has such nice friends in this, this," he paused and began glancing around the room, "this unfortunate, well—let's just say, temporary home."

Patty's hand slipped away from his firm grasp. *Did she also sense danger?*

He turned to me and smiled. "I came by today to see you, and you won't even speak to me?" he interrogated.

I turned away again and did not move.

"The doctor wants you to talk to me, Sarah." His voice took on a serious tone. I made no effort to respond and he continued, "You know, I have been very worried about you. We only want the best for you, for you to get well."

Uncle Joseph continued to speak although I didn't listen to his words. Patty got up. The nurse had called her to the counter. Patty then sauntered to the hallway on the left side of the room. On the way she glanced back at me and made a gesture of good luck, crossing her fingers; I didn't know what she meant. Uncle Joseph had put his arm around me, and I froze. After about a minute, he suddenly got up and followed Patty into the left hallway.

They both had been gone a few minutes and I began to worry. *Why did he go to the same hallway as Patty? Was he talking to her? Was she safe with him?* I turned to Bobby. He too, seemed concerned, but I couldn't talk. I couldn't even ask him what he thought. I was too frightened to move, and so I waited.

I watched the big clock on the wall. Five minutes passed, then ten. Except for watching the clock, both Bobby's and my eyes remained like sentries, never leaving their post, guarding the hallway where they had both disappeared. Finally, the door swung open and out walked Patty. I glanced back at Bobby and we both were relieved.

Patty walked up to us quickly and whispered in my ear, "I want you to come with me and listen to what I was just listening to."

Patty lifted me up, then practically pulled me across the room. I didn't want to go into that hallway and stopped. Patty turned and noticed the fear on my face. "I'm sorry Sarah, I'll go by myself. You sit down and wait for me. Don't worry, I'll be right back."

I did as she said. Bobby appeared puzzled and asked with his slur, "Whandt's wong?"

I raised my shoulders, shrugging 'I don't know.' We both just set our eyes back on the hallway, like sentries awaiting our friend to reappear. Five minutes passed by ever so slowly and I began praying that my Uncle brought no harm to Patty when out came Uncle Joseph and Dr. Frizz-brain! *What is my uncle doing with him?* I wondered.

They exchanged a handshake, smiled in a businesslike way, and Uncle Joseph went to the front door. Just before he exited, he turned and looked right at me. Hastily, I lowered my head. When I finally raised my head Uncle Joseph was gone but I noticed Dr. Frizz-brain walking from the hall to the nurse at the counter. While the two of them were talking, the nurse glanced at me. The doctor then left. *Where is Patty?* I worried. I almost got up enough courage to get up and seek her out when suddenly, to my relief, she opened the hall door and walked straight to us.

"I have to talk to you," she said urgently.

"Uh, is everything, uh, I mean, did my uncle do anything or Dr. Frizz...."

"No, no, Sarah, not exactly. I'm fine. Quit worrying. Okay? Anyway, the reason that I went out to the hall was to take a phone call from my father. I was so glad to hear from him. He called all the way from New York and he's going to be coming out here very soon."

I was so happy for Patty that I gave her a hug, though I'd heard her say that her father would be coming for her soon before....

She gave me a large crescent smile, scanned the room, and then said, "Let's go outside Sarah.

Bobby, we'll be right back."

Bobby nodded and Patty and I walked arm-in-arm into the sunny courtyard. We walked by the mad old man, who stood in that same position of his, arms outstretched. The woman who'd been visiting him was walking away, apparently disappointed.

When we got to the far side of the lawn, away from everyone else, I turned in the direction of the old man and he was looking right at me. The smile on his face seemed so pleasant and kind, and all I could do was smile back.

Patty and I sat down in the warm sun. She held both of my hands and didn't look at me right away until she finally blurted out, "Sarah, I'm not sure if I like your uncle very much."

"What do you mean?" I became anxious again. "I thought he didn't bother...."

"No, it's not that...it's just that when I got off the phone, I could hear your uncle and the doctor speaking. I heard your name and I thought I would listen for just a second. Well, I couldn't believe what I heard, so I decided to keep the phone up to my ear, just in case anyone wondered what I was doing there, and that way listened to everything I could."

"What did you hear?" I asked.

"I heard," Patty hesitated a moment, "this is so hard."

I swallowed, pressing her to go on.

"Here goes..." she stared at the lawn in front of us. "The doctor was talking about your treatments. He told your uncle that you had completed your series of them, totaling twenty-one! Wow, Sarah, I'm sorry, I hadn't realized that you'd had so many."

Patty turned to me and smiled gently. Her comforting eyes appeared to understand what I myself had difficulty grasping.

"Don't worry Sarah, I want you to know that I have a plan," she assured me. "Well anyway, your uncle seemed angry with the doctor, like he wasn't pleased with your progress. I thought that was courageous of him, you know. I mean to be able to stand up to the great Dr. Frizz-brain himself. Then, Dr. Frizz-brain assured him that he had done a sufficient job, but if your uncle wasn't satisfied, he could do more treatments along with psychotherapy. He continued on and on, saying something about the hospital being understaffed."

I was confused and asked, "What do you think this means, Patty? I don't understand."

"I don't know. Why would your uncle want you to have more treatments? Just because you wouldn't speak to him?" she wondered.

"I really don't remember him or that I even had an uncle," I told her. It's so strange. I feel all mixed up. I wanted to ask about Grandmother, but for some reason I was too scared to say anything to him and I don't know why.

"Maybe that's it!" she exclaimed.

Patty was biting her lip, all caught up in the drama, but I was the one having real turmoil. I began to fall into a hole, a deep dark place.

Patty proceeded, "I waited until after they left the room across the hall from where I was. I had to come and tell you what I heard. We have to do something!" She suddenly stopped and looked at me urgently.

"Oh, I'm sorry Sarah; you look like you've been sentenced to death. No, I don't mean that, I mean—oh, listen to me I'm just talking way too much." Patty put her arms around me and gave me a big hug. "Don't worry Sarah, we'll figure something out, I know we will. Everything will be alright, I promise. I'll write to my dad. He'll know what to do."

I still couldn't think of what to say or do. I was upset and confused. It was as if my life had been superimposed with a life I didn't know existed. "What happened to me?" I agonized.

Patty assured me that she had a plan. However, I just wanted to run away.

"Let's go back inside. I'm sure Bobby is worried," Patty said.

On the way back we passed by the old man again. He was smiling and conducting his slow-motion movements. He seemed to be so much at peace unlike Katharine or anyone else here, including me.

Patty explained to Bobby what had happened and some of her ideas. Afterwards, we sat silently for a long while. Patty appeared in quiet contemplation; Bobby even looked like he was going to come up with something to help while I just sat there while fear pressed in on me.

After a while, Patty piped up, "Listen Sarah. I want you to know that there is hope. I have the best solution! We have to convince Dr. Frizz-brain and your uncle that you don't need any more treatments." Patty grabbed my hand firmly. "We have to get you even better!" she insisted. "Your uncle thinks that you don't remember him, so we need to work on that memory of yours! Once you remember your uncle; things will start looking up and you won't need any more of those stupid treatments!" Then she added, "Oh, and another thing is that I *will* get my dad to help. I am certain. So, you see we have a few great ideas to work on. I'll hash it over and see you at dinner.

I don't want you to give it a second thought. Okay, Sarah?"

I gave her a slight smile in acknowledgment, even though I felt hopeless and confused. At least there was one thing to hope for but even then, I really didn't want to think about what my future might bring. We parted and I decided to go outside and spy on that curious old man.

I sat on a bench by the big wall that the cloak of afternoon shadows hadn't touched. With my back leaning up against the wall, I lifted my gown just to my knees to bathe my thin legs in the sunlight. The man was still dancing his slow movements as if he were pushing the air with his hands creating invisible designs, almost like frosting a cake. I enjoyed watching his slow, mesmerizing movements and they, in turn, started to make me feel sleepy. I thought about what Patty said about my needing to remember this uncle, but I didn't want to remember him, I wanted to remember Jimmy. As I was dozing off, I felt myself drifting away from the stark realities that surrounded me and falling into a place of lost memories.

The Blessing

A nother day of dashed hopes. Another day filled with tears. Haven't I cried enough?

Stupid stars!"

I close my diary shutting it tight as if doing so will change or squeeze out all the pain and suffering I have had to endure. Another tear drops onto my diary. Why did Jimmy have to move anyway? It's not fair! It's not fair at all!

A week ago, I watched a team of big men pile box after box into the large moving truck. Jimmy was so busy packing since he got back from Los Angeles; we could only steal a few minutes with each other. Even then, we had little to say. I think that we were both sad. He would glance up at my window, but I couldn't bear to see him leave so I just sat by in silence.

Right before they left, Jimmy came over to say goodbye. Nan yelled upstairs for me to come and see him. I peeked around the corner and peered downstairs. There was Jimmy talking with Nan near the parlor. He kept glancing upstairs out of the corner of his eye. He was waiting for me. Nan yelled for the second time, "Sarah, come and say au revoir to Jimmy!"

I finally got up the courage and walked ever so slowly, grasping the rail tight, one step at a time.

Jimmy watched me the whole way.

I couldn't say much. Neither could Jimmy. He talked about how they were going to live with his grandparents and that the grandparents needed them. He didn't know for how long they'd stay with his relatives. In my anguish I blurted out, "Why can't you just stay here?!" But as soon as those desperate words left my lips, I realized how silly they were. I could see that Jimmy was sad and that I wasn't making it any easier for him. He said he would write, but it's been a week and I haven't gotten a letter. Nan said that men or boys don't write much and not to expect anything. She gave me a big hug and I cried in her arms after the truck pulled away…away for good.

I don't think I'll ever be the same. No, never.

I walk to my closet and pull out the dress we bought in San Francisco for the dance. I hold it up, pressing it in front of me and stare into my full-length mirror. It's a pale blue chiffon with ever so tiny white dots. They remind me of stars as if seen in the daylight. My hand touches the tiny waist. I love how it's just right on my hips and then gathers with a full skirt. And a little to the left side is a small bow. I gently tap the slightly puffed sleeves and gaze wistfully. The sleeves aren't short or long, they are in-between. Grandmother called them ¾ lengths. I put my hand over my heart and feel the scoop neck with tiny gathers and a small bow on the right. It's the prettiest dress I've ever had. Both Grandmother and Nan said I should still go to the dance with a girlfriend, but they took just one look at me and realized the error in such assumptions. The very thought of going without Jimmy… besides, the dance was on the same day that Jimmy had to leave. I just couldn't.

Two gentle taps sound on my door. "Sarah?" says Nan.

"Oui," I answer. Quickly, I put away my dress and shut the closet door. Nan comes in with my glass of warm milk.

"Mon Dieu! Why aren't you in bed?

I walk to my bed, throw back the coverlet and climb in, wearily. "No reason," I answer.

"Remember that you are my helper tomorrow…at least for the morning. I know that Grandmother needs you too. Father Carl will be at the vineyard for the blessing at 11 A.M. and then everyone will come here afterwards for the feast."

"I know, I know." I sigh. "You've told me time and again!"

Nan is quiet for a moment. I try not to look up at her. But she says, "Oh, before I forget, I want you to do one more thing in the morning."

"What?" I answer a little sharply.

"Cut some roses from our garden. I know how you love to do that, Sarah."

I soften my tone and say, "Oui, Nan. Of course, I will."

Just before Nan closes my door behind her, I offer her, "Bonne nuit, Nan."

"Bonne nuit, my little one." She says soothingly.

In the morning, I awaken early to the constant chirp of busy birds and the first sun piercing my room. I glance over at my window and realize that I didn't put away my diary and that I feel an urge to write. Just for a bit, I think. I know there is much to do.

So, I begin:

Saturday morning, May 7, 1938

"He's gone.

My window seat is my haven. My diary is a reflection of that haven (I really like that word…haven). Also, the words that I write and thoughts that I formulate in my diary give me a comfortable feeling of safety and I think that it has become my most sacred haven—a place I can go to, without interruption and consequences, only of my doing. Sometimes, writing is like painting a picture, which I want to do too."

Birds chirp. I look out at the trees; several are flying from branch to branch. I watch them quietly until words form again.

"Wind is an emotion moving the trees to-and-fro. Sun sparkles through the full green leaves like reflections of light shimmering on the lake. Why do I feel so alone? I know that I miss Jimmy terribly, but this is a different and strange feeling that haunts me. Even the reason for feeling lonely seems empty.

Maybe, I'm just learning what alone actually is. Empty. I wonder if anyone else feels like me. Do the trees ache because they cannot reach out to other trees or cry because they get their branches blown off in a storm?"

The aroma of simmering garlic drifts up on the breeze and into my window. I decide it must be time for me to help Nan with preparations for the blessing party.

I stare at my fountain pen, my deckle-edged white paper and leather-bound diary, then place the pen to paper for one last thought.

"The process of writing makes me think of a field filled with clumps of dirt and writing is the tiller that makes all the rows line up for planting."

Sighing, I close my diary carefully and place my hand on the cover. Gazing out through the windowpanes, I conclude that I can feel the change happening in my life because I feel compelled to write. However, just like the wind, life is always changing. I look out at Jimmy's yard. It seems so empty, except for the birds! I wonder if he'll ever come back. I wonder who will live there if he doesn't.

"Bang!" the kitchen door swings open.

"Mon Dieu! Nan shouts. "Why do you burst through doors like the bull out of the pen?"

"I'm sorry, Nan," I say. "What can I do to help you?"

Nan chides me with a quick glare then proceeds to stir the pot, chewing on her thoughts.

"I know!" I say. "I'll cut the roses."

"Bon," she says. "The vases are on the table. Use the basket," she adds, as I dart out the back door.

"I know, I know," I answer.

The screen door slams behind me and I hear Nan yelling from the kitchen, "Mon Dieu!"

"Sorry!" I shout back.

In the shed are the clippers, the basket and gloves. I always wear gloves when cutting roses because whenever the thorns scratch me, my skin itches. No matter how much I protect myself, the thorns always manage to pierce my gloves or find my unprotected skin!

I think about Jimmy and realize that I have been left with the sting of another type of thorn.

I scour the front garden for the best roses. We have a beautiful arbor arching over the entryway to our garden. Red and pink roses, mostly in full bloom, blanket the bush. However, I am on the hunt for longer stems and roses that are just slightly open for our beautiful crystal vases. It's good to replace a hurt heart with purposeful action and beauty.

After successfully collecting almost a full basket of roses without a scratch, I go to my favorite bush on the south side of our garden. It glows with the most fragrant deep yellow-gold roses. They always make me feel happy as if they have soaked up the warmth of a sunny day as if this warmth is just to be shared with me.

I clip the easy ones on the outside of the bush first, and then reach deeply into the middle trying to clip the longest stem and at the same time I don't want the thorns to prick me. Just when I'm about to clip another rose, a strange and uneasy feeling passes through me and I become distracted. "Ouch! Not again!" I yell at myself and pull away.

I pull off my glove and begin sucking on my bleeding finger. When I do, I notice a black car parked across the street. I know every family's car on our block and I've never seen this car before. It sort of looks like the McAllister's car but older. Suddenly, I see fingertips at the driver's window holding up a lit cigarette. I cannot see a face and the hand almost appears bodiless. The hand draws back into the car and then out again. Now, the lit tip glows red and smoke drifts out of the window.

I turn to my basket and then back again at the car when the strangest feeling passes through me. I decide that I have enough roses for now and go back into the kitchen. Just before I go around the corner, I glance back at the car once more. Whoever it is, they are still there.

I burst through the side door. "Nan, there's a strange man in a strange car across the street. He's just sitting there, smoking a cigarette."

"What beautiful roses you cut," Nan says.

"Nan, didn't you hear me? There's a strange man across the street!"

Nan looks at me curiously. She knows me well enough and can sense my concern.

Attempting to allay it she says, "I'm sure there's nothing to worry about. People come and go on the street all the time."

"But this is different. I just know it is. Can't you just please look?" I plead.

Stubbornly, "I tell you it is nothing."

Shouldn't we at least tell Grandmother?"

"Non, mon petit. She is in the library. Let's not disturb her just yet. The man is just having a smoke. Maybe his wife doesn't like him to smoke. Who knows? He will probably leave in a minute."

I grab her hand, and say, "Come here with me," and take her to the front parlor.

We both go to the window and look outside. The street is empty.

"It was there just a minute ago," I contend.

"Oh, my dear, you have such an imagination! But you see? It's all as I expected and I'm sure there was nothing to worry about."

"It was a black car," I insist, "just sitting there… Maybe it's someone wanting to move into Jimmy's house. They said that they would rent it out for now."

Nan looks down at me, "They may be renters. Who knows? As for now, I have much to do. Can you arrange the flowers for me?"

"Yes, Nan, I will," I say, though I still feel uneasy about the man in the black sedan.

Nan walks back into the kitchen while I begin my arrangements at the dining room table. First, I place newspapers down on the table and cut off the thorns and carefully break some of the large ones off with my thumb and forefinger and put them in their own pile. Then I sort out three bunches for the three vases, each with one dominating color along with a variety of the other colors to mix it up.

Every so often, I go into the parlor and peer out of the window to see if the car has come back, though it doesn't; then I return to my task of carefully arranging each bouquet. Once I am done, though, I feel drawn to look out one last time. The car still isn't there. Finally, I give up and conclude that it is probably a good thing.

Nan loves the arrangements. "You always do that so wonderfully!" she praises me.

Just before 11:00 AM Grandmother, Nan, Dr. Simpson, Father Carl, Roberto, all the workers and I are standing in the new vineyard for the annual blessing and prayers for all our grape vines. It is a beautiful day. The sky is bright blue with white fluffy clouds that slowly stream by. Everyone is chatting and catching up with each other. The blessing is a centuries-old ceremony to ensure the harvest will be plentiful, the wine good, and the vineyard field workers safe throughout the season.

As Father Carl begins the first prayer, we bow our heads in silence. He offers a prosperity prayer and then begins the many blessings. Father Carl walks slowly down the rows sprinkling Holy Water on the vines and earth. He blesses the future harvest. Then he walks up to everyone and blesses all the field workers and all who are there, while sprinkling us with Holy Water.

When he finishes, we all make the sign of the cross.

Afterwards, everyone comes to our house for the feast. The food is generous, and everyone applauds Nan repeatedly for her wonderful dishes and fancy desserts. I frequently had to go down to the basement for more desserts and more wine! I enjoy having so many people here as it makes me feel less lonely for Jimmy, but I do wish he were here to enjoy the feast with us.

When the festivities wind down, I help Nan with the task of tidying up. The field workers put away the extra chairs and tables while some of the women help in the kitchen. I enjoy seeing them laughing while they wash and dry dishes, pots and pans as Nan makes sure they put everything away in the right place without breaking anything! There is so much commotion. I am merely in the way, so I decide to go and find Grandmother.

She is out on the veranda with Dr. Simpson sharing a bottle of her best vintage. She sees me walk out. "Sarah, come here dear," she says.

When I sit down, she offers me a small glass of wine. I wait for the dilution, but she offers none. "That's strange," I think, and then take a sip. It is very good. I think she knows that I would appreciate it better without the water. She looks at me and I nod with high approval. Our silence speaks volumes.

Dr. Simpson on the other hand is full of words. "Annabelle," he begins, drawing back Grandmother's attention, "What do you think about Hitler taking over Austria?"

"Well, Doctor, I am glad that we are not living in Europe right now," she says.

"Yes, this is true. But I heard rumors that they will be confiscating the fortunes of the Jews," he adds.

"Oh, I don't think so," said Grandmother.

"Remember Annabelle, I have friends in Germany. It is not public knowledge. What is happening there must be stopped!"

Grandmother notices, as do I, that Dr. Simpson appears as though his blood pressure were rising, and he's old. She diverts his attention to matters at hand. "Dr. Simpson, would you like a good Cuban cigar?"

Dr. Simpson's eyes light up. He smiles. Grandmother turns to me and I immediately know what to do. I go into the parlor where she keeps her prize cigar box. I return with a metal tray that holds the box, a lighter, the cigar cutter and a heavy dark-green glass ashtray, all implements that Grandmother has had for a very long time. My Grandfather used them all. Grandmother subtly diverted the fiery conversation to a discussion with a different fire; a proper cigar, how to light one and who produces the best.

We are quietly, yet continuously, interrupted by our guests leaving and thanking Grandmother for her hospitality. I finish my small glass of wine that I sipped and savored ever so slowly and begin to feel the busyness of the day catch up with me—and possibly the effect of the alcohol made me a little drowsy. The sun has set and most everyone has left. I bid my goodnight to Grandmother and Dr. Simpson. When I stand, he stands also and wishes me good evening.

As I walk away, I feel a bit more grown up and that I am becoming increasingly a part of that world. It makes me feel good, warm within and not a little mellow. I go into the kitchen to say goodnight to Nan. She is propping up her head with her palm cupping her chin and elbow resting firmly on the table. In her other hand, is her glass of wine! I softly giggle at the scene of her exhaustion and congratulate her on the successful festivities of the day because of all her hard work. I give her a big hug and bid her, "Bonne nuit, Nan."

Nan smiles and thanks me. She gifts me with a wide smile. "Bonne nuit!" she says as I leave to go to bed.

The Confirmation

Present

B arbara was due any minute. I hope she doesn't have too much trouble with getting here. I walked over to peer out the front window. The rain returned in the middle of the night and hadn't ceased.

Just then I noticed Barbara running up the drive with her umbrella overhead protecting her from the heavy onslaught. I quickly opened the door.

"Do you believe this?" I laughed.

"The weather's becoming normal around here, almost like Seattle," she grinned sardonically, shaking the wet coat out at the entrance and putting her umbrella in the stand.

I took her coat and said, "Why don't you have a seat. I'll hang it in the back near a heat register and get us some coffee." As I left the room I shouted, "Did you hear? They said that the snow could get down to sea level!"

"Yes," she voiced. "But I doubt it."

"We're practically at sea level!" I shouted, reaching for a cup in the cupboard.

"Nah, I very much doubt it," she shouted back.

I began to think about the fog we have and our in a valley as I walked into the living room with our coffee.

"The fog this time of year is usually so damp and cold—the kind of dampness that seeps right in, chilling me to the bone. I think I'd rather have snow," I said. "At least then there'd be some excuse for the chill!"

I sat down and lit a few candles on my coffee table. Despite the sound of rain, the room was quiet, warm and comfortably enclosed. I put my feet up on the divan, sipped coffee from my red mug and settled in for the visit. Barbara reached into her satchel and pulled out the section.

"I read each chapter," she began, at the same time placing her hand on top of the stack, patting it gently. "It's quite amazing to me that you even remember all this. I wrote some questions that came up, like you suggested and made a few corrections." She handed me the questions written on a small sheet of paper.

I read the first one out loud, "'Where did this happen Sarah?'" A simple, even logical question. But though it made sense, I wasn't really prepared for her to call *me* Sarah. I realized that her calling me Sarah raised the hair on the back of my neck. Emotion welled up in my throat. For just a second, I had to lift my head, turn away. I looked out at the window, at the wall of rain, like tears rimming. Barbara waited, her patience an audible presence in the room. I focused on the scrap of paper in my hand and resumed reading, stating the question more quietly this time. Where did this happen Sarah? I felt the walls close in with the silence and the rain. The handle of the coffee cup seemed heavy in my grip. The wall clock seemed to tick louder. Where to begin? I thought, and then looked across at her.

"Yes," Barbara said, quietly. "Can you remember?"

I glanced down again while thinking of what to tell her. "Just a minute," I said, leaning forward and setting the mug in its coaster. "Give me a second." Barbara smiled and relaxed back on the sofa waiting patiently.

"As far as I can recall it was Napa State Hospital." As the words left my mouth, I felt a returning uneasiness. I sensed that I was getting myself into trouble.

She looked at me with a register of shock at the name of the institution. Then asked, "What's wrong?"

I hesitated a moment, had a slight giggle, shook my head and said, "It's just that...I still can't believe that talking about where it took place affects me like this."

"Of course it does. I understand."

"Believe it or not, I went there in 1984 with some friends just to drive through the grounds."

"God," she breathed. "You did? My goodness." Barbara put her hand on my arm, lightly, warm with sympathy.

"It's strange isn't it?" I began, moved by tears, drifting back again to earlier feelings. "This whole thing is so far removed, like a fictional novel, yet at the same time all too real." I shook my head, trying to throw it off. "Strange, isn't it?"

"Strange is as strange seems," she said, with gentle humor.

"You're funny."

She paused a moment then asked, "So you mentioned that you visited the hospital in '84? Why then?"

"In 1984 it was more of a curiosity. At the time, the idea had just popped into my head and I followed through with a visit to the site—which I've realized happens with me quite often. It had also been seven years since I'd had the counseling sessions, and the memories were watered down by time. Basically, I was curious. My great fault."

"Isn't that what got you into this in the first place," she commented.

I grabbed a muffin arrayed along with others on the plate on my coffee table, looked up at Barbara, bit, chewed and swallowed a bite and said, "Yes, of course. I wrote about my adventure of going there and wasn't sure when I was going to have you read it but now seems like a good time."

"Really?! I'd love to read it. I'm sure it's fascinating"

"Of course, you would," I said with a knowing look, and then shook my head. "I'll go get it." I started to get up, but an idea came to me. "I don't know if I mentioned that I have more pertinent stories. I've also finished writing from my present life things that I plan on sharing with you as they are relevant to chapters in Sarah's story."

"Like what?"

"A lot of synchronicity—how I discovered I'm psychic and the journey of that discovery.

Also, I have several miracles."

"I can't wait," she said.

"Me too. Those stories are the antithesis to the horrors Sarah experienced." I smiled, sighed, got up and retrieved the story. "Here you are," I said, handing it over to her. "You can read it while I clean up the kitchen, a never-ending chore. It will take some time to read. Hopefully not too long," I added.

She gave me a quick look, set her coffee cup down and said, "Thank you."

Barbara was excited to find out about my journey into my past and immediately turned to the first page as I stepped away.

The Journey

July 1984
My Journal

Bill and I had moved twice since we were in the apartment above the garages. One was just before our first daughter, Carissa, was born and the second was about a year after the birth of our second daughter, Lara. Several circumstances allowed our family to move into the house that Bill grew up in. His mother, a wonderful woman, unfortunately passed away suddenly when Lara was a newborn and his father, who was always generous and wanted to help, had moved in with a friend.

We had three bedrooms, a nice yard in a quiet neighborhood, and neighbors that Bill had known his entire life.

It was a typical Saturday morning. Bill left earlier to umpire a softball tournament and the kids had just finished breakfast. I was washing the dishes.

I looked out of the kitchen window wondering how long our heat wave would last and prayed that the Delta Breeze would cool us down this evening, but I doubted it. It was already 85 degrees and it's been well over 100 degrees for 6 days now.

Familiar sounds of Saturday morning cartoons blaring suddenly. I wiped my hands and walked into the family room.

My two little girls, just two and five, were sitting on the floor completely hypnotized by the TV. "Do you have to have it so loud?" I pleaded.

Lara did not move. Her eyes remained glazed and focused on the TV, totally entranced by Scooby Doo's antics. Carissa, my "little adult" five-year-old, glanced up and immediately pushed the sound button on the remote, "Is that better, Mommy?"

"Yes sweetie. Thank you."

As I went back to finish the dishes, I began reminiscing about my own Saturday mornings almost 30 years ago and how I stayed glued to the TV for hours just like my girls! My sister Valerie and I would laugh aloud at Bugs Bunny or The Road Runner every Saturday morning. However, when I thought of my all-time favorite, "The Mickey Mouse Club", my head started bobbing back and forth. I began putting away the dishes to the tune in my head, "Hey there! Hi there! Ho there! You're as welcome as can be. M, I, C, see you real soon, K, E, Y. Why? Because we like you. M, O, U, S, E."

For me, the pinnacle of the show was when Tommy, Jimmy, Annette, or another Mouseketeer would smile and walk over to a wooden chest of drawers with a look that meant something unheralded was about to happen as soon as they opened it. Even though another cartoon would suddenly appear, I always expected the show to transport me to a place I had never seen before. Each week I never lost that expectation.

While stacking another plate into the cupboard, I suddenly felt a familiar tug. A yearning—ever since I was sixteen—to write down thoughts, ideas and imaginings.

I smiled as I walked past my beautiful girls still glued to the TV thinking how they are enjoying themselves just as I did. I went to my bedroom where I kept my journal and sat on my bed. When I reached for the handle of my top dresser drawer, I suddenly realized that every time I wrote I felt the same tantalizing expectation I had as a child when a Mouseketeer slid open the drawer.

When I am contemplating what to write, I transport myself to this magical world first by pondering a thought and then gaze into the unknown until new thoughts are born. I've loved journaling since I was sixteen and when I feel that urge, I know that something important to me will appear as I write. While looking in one of my dresser drawers for an empty notebook I came across a small one and opened it up.

In my handwriting was one page of a story I had stated. It described the front garden and neighborhood around my home from what I recalled as Sarah.

Since recalling that life I had a notion it would be an interesting story and here was one of my few attempts to begin. I shook my head and thought why do I never get past one page?

As my mind turned over the multitude of images from my memories an idea came to me. Something I had never considered. As this idea formed, I came up with a plan and someone to help me. I didn't want to do this alone.

I went to the phone and called my friend.

"Hello," said Debbie.

I was surprised she was home as she is always busy. "Hi, Deb, you're actually home!"

After chatting a bit, on blind courage I asked, "Hey Deb…remember that past life I mentioned to you a few years ago?"

"The one where we were both Flapper girls in Chicago?" She laughed.

"No, not that one," I said and then quipped, "that's one I'm not so certain about!"

"Which one then?"

"The one where I was a young girl in a mental institution. Do you remember?"

"Yes, I remember."

"Well, an idea just came to me."

Debbie asked hesitantly, "What?"

"I was thinking about going there to find out if my memories are accurate."

"Where?" she asked.

"Napa."

Debbie sighed. "I love Napa…Sounds like fun. So, do you have an idea where you lived?"

"Not exactly, but I do know that the house was a big Victorian." I hesitated a moment before mentioning, "However there is a place I want to check out."

"What's that?"

I took in a deep breath, and then spoke. "To the hospital…Napa State Hospital."

Debbie questioned, "You wanna actually go there?" and then chuckled. "Only you, Kerry!"

Most people who know about Napa State Hospital have heard something about its scary reputation. It is a large hospital for the mentally ill and criminally insane, which opened in 1875 to relieve the overcrowded Stockton Asylum.

I stated, "Yes and no, actually. I just want to see it. I have images in my mind of what I will see. I think it'll be interesting."

"You always come up with something!" she joked. "Sure, I'll go with you."

After we made plans two weeks out for our excursion into my past, we said our goodbyes. In one way, I was relieved that I had a plan. On the other hand, I began to wonder if my memories would prove to be wrong.

Then a chill ran through my core when I said under my breath, "What if it is all true? What then?"

The Accident

I called Debbie the Thursday before we were to go on our outing to Napa. Raj, Debbie's boyfriend, answered and gave me devastating news. Deb's father was missing! He was boating in Bodega Bay when a huge wave came up and capsized the boat. He said that Deb and her family had been there several times however the search team hadn't found him.

I told Raj to let Debbie know how sorry I was and that I would pray for her and her family. He said that he would let her know and that I called.

After we hung up, I prayed for Debbie's father, Debbie and her family. I thought about my father and the tragedy surrounding his death and felt what she must be going through. Even though I wanted to offer her some comfort, all I could do was be patient for her to return my call. In the meantime, something quite peculiar happened.

The following day was my dear mother's (Yvonne) birthday. We were having a family dinner at her home. My immediate family was all there; Tom, my older brother, his wife Rayanne and their kids, Valerie and her kids, Bill, our kids and me.

The sounds of forks and knives tapping plates, laughter and multiple conversations resonated around the dining room table. During a lull, I decided to share the tragic news I heard a few days before.

I turned to Valerie. "You remember my friend Debbie?"

"Yes, I think I've met her a few times," she said. "Why?"

"Well, her father was boating in Bodega Bay when a huge wave came up suddenly and capsized his boat."

My mother, who heard the story earlier, chimed in, "Her father is still missing."

"That's terrible," Rayanne said.

"I know. It's awful. I can't imagine what Debbie is going through right now. They've been there several times, hoping the search would turn up something."

I glanced at Valerie who hadn't said anything. Her hand was on her chest and her face lost color.

"What's wrong?" I asked.

Valerie could barely look at anyone. Finally, she turned to me and said, "I had a dream. It was last night. I was a man in a small silver boat. It capsized." Tears formed in her eyes.

"Are you alright, Valerie?"

"I don't know. I'm all right, I guess. It's just weird. I don't really know Debbie and I've never met her father." She looked at me. "Do you think I saw his accident? I think that's what it was! I think I saw his accident."

Everyone began talking at once and asking her questions, but Valerie remained quiet. She was stunned. Usually, I was the one having weird experiences. Now Valerie was.

Rayanne spoke up. "Maybe he was communicating to you. I've heard that people who die sometimes find someone receptive."

Valerie spoke, "Yes, I've heard that, and I have heard it can come in a dream."

"What else do you remember, Valerie?" I asked.

"I remember being on the ocean in a silver boat. A large wave flipped the boat over, and I was under water and couldn't breathe."

"What do you mean, *you*?"

"I was the man." She put her head down. "It was awful."

I asked softly, "Do you know what he looked like?"

Valerie closed her eyes. "He's older. He had on a blue-plaid shirt and jeans." She began to sob quietly.

"Oh, my goodness," I said. "Are you okay?"

"It feels like *I'm* the one that died," Valerie managed to say.

Everyone was in a state of not knowing exactly what to make of what just transpired. Valerie calmed down and in a little while, we were able to go on with the festivities. Later on, I mentioned to Valerie that I would call Debbie and tell her about the dream in hopes that we would find some answers. She seemed very relieved. Something about this dream was important.

A few days later Debbie called me back. We talked about how she and her family were coping. She said that they had been there several times hoping for a miracle. After we talked a while, I asked her what kind of boat her father had.

When she said, "a silver boat," I felt that it was time to tell her about Valerie's dream.

When I recounted the dream to her, she was surprised and very curious. She wanted to know if Valerie had described the man. I told her what my sister said, but when I mentioned what he wore, Debbie said that she would have to ask her brother. Apparently, her brother and sister-in-law were also in the boat but managed to swim to a rock island and someone rescued them. She said that when she saw her brother next time, she would ask him what her father was wearing. She also wanted to bring over a photo of her dad to show Valerie. Did Valerie really see her father? Both of us were eager to unravel the mystery of her dream.

The next day Debbie brought over a photo of her father. She talked about how strange it was that he worked for Water Resources and was around water his whole life. He loved the water… and he loved fishing. She also mentioned something strange that happened to her the last time she saw him.

"I went to see him at his office, and I didn't know that he decided to let his hair go completely gray. I was shocked. But something else was strange." Debbie stopped and recalled that moment.

"What?" I asked.

"I know this may sound weird," she began, "but I saw a glow around him. Immediately, I went over to him, gave him a hug and told him that I loved him. He was surprised by my sudden show of affection and said he loved me too."

"That's amazing, Debbie! What do you think that meant?"

"At the time I didn't know what to think, but now I believe that it meant he was going to die, and I was supposed to see him that one last time."

"Oh, my goodness."

"Know what else? I was talking to a neighbor and mentioned what happened that last time I saw him, and she too saw a strange glow and had a similar feeling just before the accident."

"Well, something is trying to tell you that he is alright."

"Yes, I know that."

After we talked about the continuing search for her father, and how she had made several trips there, I had an idea. "Deb. Do you still want to go with me to Napa?"

"Yes, I do."

"What do you think about Valerie coming with us and after we visit Napa, we could go to Bodega Bay? We could make a day of it."

"Yes! Let's go next weekend."

In the meantime, I showed Valerie the photo of Deb's father. Valerie became quite emotional again and stared at the photo in awe. "This looks like the man I saw Kerry, except his hair was gray."

Then, I shared with her Debbie's story about when she saw her father with his hair suddenly gray. Valerie was stunned. "Know what else?"

"What?"

"When Debbie talked to her brother, she asked him what her father was wearing that day. He said, 'a blue-plaid shirt and jeans,' your exact words!"

"Really?" she asked as she wiped her eyes.

I nodded and then went on to tell her how Debbie and I wanted her to come with us on our outing to Napa and Bodega. Valerie agreed and suggested that Rayanne join us as well.

After she left, I thought how strange it was that Debbie and I were searching for answers for two tragedies forty years apart; my own death in a previous life and her missing father. I felt as if I was stepping into an unknown world and had absolutely no idea what would happen.

The Windowed Wall

The moist breeze cooled my face as I stared out of the rear car window. We were slowly passing jail-like dormitory buildings and I had a fleeting sense of being in suspended animation. Clouds, in shades of dark gray-blue to white, dotted the sky creating dancing shadows on the landscape that shifted moods from ominous to hope and back again. The constant wet sound of tires rolling over damp streets from the recent downpour provided a sense of familiar continuity to this less familiar destination. For now, it has stopped raining.

Valerie, my brave and curious sister was our navigator. She was leaning forward, tightly gripping the steering wheel while navigating through the expansive, old hospital grounds. Rayanne, my sister-in-law, was the co-pilot and Debbie was next to me in the back seat.

I could easily imagine what we must look like. All of us were gawking and apprehensive yet trying to act as if we knew what we were doing and had a specific destination. After all, we had no "legitimate" reason to be driving through the grounds; we knew no employees or any of the patients. We were merely driving around somewhat aimlessly, hoping for anything that struck a chord with me.

The past hour's journey quickly flashed in my mind. On the way to Napa State Hospital, Debbie watched me as I sketched out memories from my past life, after which she'd openly question with strong disbelief if I really expected those things to be there. All I had were visual and visceral memories, so I would just shrug my shoulders and say that was what I remembered.

I drew the perspective of a long drive with a large castle-like building at the other end and a fountain. I drew tennis courts surrounded by tall fir trees. I also sketched a hint of sprawling lawns, long dormitories and the infamous 'windowed wall'. I quickly added a few more sketches as I described beautiful gardens and noted that there was something to do with a tuberculosis ward. I mentioned to Debbie that I wasn't sure if I had it or what. She scoffed at the concept of tennis courts in a mental hospital and tall fir trees; after all, the hospital was in the fertile Napa Valley, not the mountains.

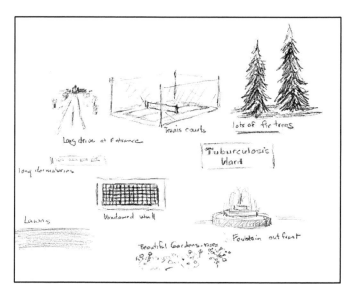

The first thing we saw when we turned off the highway was the long drive with a large building at the end just as I drew. Debbie was shocked. "Are you certain you were never here?"

I rolled my eyes, half-joking, and said, "Not in this life."

I was disappointed that there was no fountain or colorful flowers, but it was easy to surmise from the dilapidation of the one hundred-year-old grounds that after forty-three years since I was there—In a completely different life—that everything was rundown. The building did seem smaller than what I remembered but I figured it was probably because I was not a grown woman the last time "I" was here.

When we neared the expansive building, everyone's jaws dropped with what was on the right side! Debbie blurted out, "Look, there are tennis courts and fir trees! I never expected to see either!" She laughed in amazement and shook her head.

I would have preferred to be wrong.

As the past hour had caught up with me, I realized that the journey thus far rapidly deflated my original enthusiasm leaving me feeling emotionally drained. I glanced down at my sketchbook and had no desire to draw anything else.

The road curved and we began heading back towards where we entered, except we were now on the backside of the complex. As we continued around the fortress, we saw graffiti on one of the walls in large red letters that read, "Satan lives here". Everyone turned towards me expecting some sort of "ah ha" moment but I didn't have one. I thought it strange though that the sign particularly frightened my sister; she talked about it many times after.

Once we passed the jail-like buildings, we came across an incongruous park-like setting with well-manicured green lawns canopied by many trees and roads going all different ways. Valerie randomly picked one and continued to drive slowly.

On the other side of the park area, we came upon a small group of people standing near a building on the lawn in the shade. I knew by their peculiar demeanor that they were not attendants and guessed that they were self-admitted patients, as they were not confined. As the car approached, each one of them turned and stared with great curiosity at our slow-moving vehicle as if this was a highlight of their day, or any day for that matter.

I asked Valerie to hurry up because I didn't want anyone to notice us. However, she didn't take heed of my concern, continued at a snail's pace (which unnerved me) and was out of keeping with her normal driving. She was notorious for going fast and loving hot rods, but she had not driven above 15-20 MPH since we turned onto the hospital grounds. She continued, almost as if she had a real sense of where she was going; making right turns, then left turns and never stopping, just in a constant motion through the maze of roads. We passed by some open landscape dotted by trees in the rear of the grounds, and then by a firehouse—everyone but me agreed that the old firehouse was weird, to me the *whole experience was weird*—and then she made another turn and began driving between two larger buildings. By this time, I was ready to leave.

Debbie piped up, "Stop here!"

Valerie obeyed without question and pulled over on the side of the road between the two buildings.

I looked at Valerie with an expression of, "Why in the hell did you stop here?" and then displayed that same expression to Debbie. At the same moment, Valerie and Rayanne turned to find out what Debbie so urgently wanted.

"You don't have to go to the bathroom here, do you?" asked Valerie.

"No."

I looked over into the building on the left and saw what appeared to be administrative employees through the large windows. Immediately, I turned to Debbie. "I'm not about to go in there and ask about medical records from the 1930's! I just wanted to *drive through* this place."

Debbie's eyebrows raised and she tilted her head slightly as she quipped, "No...but that's not a bad idea."

I was in no mood. "Very funny," I retorted.

"Let's get out and look," encouraged Debbie with an odd enthusiasm that no one else seemed to share.

What the Hell is she thinking! "I'm not going." I pointed at my sister. "*You* go with her."

"No way!" she said. "This place gives me the creeps! 'Satan lives here', remember?"

Rayanne chimed in, "I'm not getting out of the car," and then giggled nervously.

"Come on you two!" Debbie pleaded.

In unison, they wholeheartedly said, "No!"

Valerie and Rayanne peered into the back, first looking at me, then Debbie, and then back at me wondering what was going to happen next.

She finally coaxed me out of the car 'just to look around'. I relinquished. She began walking briskly, taking the lead, and like Valerie seemed to have a sense of where she was going. This dumbfounded me. What is it with these people? I did not expect them to be active participants, after all, I just wanted to drive through the grounds, verify what I recalled as true and not go traipsing about on foot!

At this point, my past life seemed to have a gravitation of its own pulling me directly into a state of limbo. As I walked the grounds, it felt as if an aspect of me was actually going back in time to Sarah's life and death. I was not myself and I was not Sarah. Who am I really?

Once we reached the end of the building, Debbie slowed her pace and became circumspect. The sky seemed to mimic our countenance; it suddenly darkened and felt damp, as if it were going to start raining any moment. We shared a knowing look that something strange was about to take place. Rounding the corner another building a little further away came into view. It was very old, long and narrow, and looked to be an obvious housing for patients.

Debbie was again surprised with my accurate sketches of memories when she saw double doors with tiny inset windows. I wanted to rebuke with, 'So-o-o-o' but couldn't.

The sign above the door stopped us cold. It was my fifth verification, "Tuberculosis Ward". The closer we came to the building we could see that it was dilapidated and appeared not to be in use.

With devious dark eyes, Debbie said in a quiet voice, "Let's look inside."

I whispered back, "No. I don't want to."

Despite my answer, she put her hand on the door and looked straight at me. I gave in. What the hell, no one is paying any attention to what I want anyway.

Debbie slowly pulled open the old, yawning door. We peered into a dimly lit, long, empty hall that was at least 200 feet deep. The hall was wide with many doors on both sides. It was dusty, old and in disrepair.

"I'm not going in," I told her. She didn't move. An awful, eerie feeling overcame me. I could almost see the ghosts of tormented souls flying and swirling around down the long hallway and many more who would forever remain locked up in their rooms. I had an inexpressible sense that if we took one single step inside that this old ward would easily devour us as it had the long-gone patients and we too would never be able to leave.

When she looked at me, I could see she was just as afraid as I was. Without saying a word, she shut the door and we headed straight back to our waiting car. As soon as we opened the car door, Valerie and Rayanne bombarded us with a flurry of questions. What happened? What did you see?

Once we were safely in the car, Debbie answered all of the questions with complete enthusiasm about our daring exploration, the sign, the double doors with tiny inset windows and the dark, scary hallway. She held up my sketches and notations, pointing at how all of them were true. "Can you believe it? Isn't that weird?" she said repeatedly.

Yes, everything I drew and noted was there. I got what I wanted, verifications. I sat back halfway listening and at the same time slowly fell prey to the reality that six years of haunting memories of this place were real, actually real. The visceral atmosphere of this notorious mental hospital began to seep in, and forty-three-year-old screams echoed in my mind like church bells in the distance. I took in a shaky, deep breath and was more than ready to leave.

"I've seen enough Valerie. Let's go," I pleaded with her.

Valerie started the car and began driving back towards the exit. I looked to the sky. The warm sunbathed my face bringing me a sense of relief. Fluffy, white clouds surrounded by crisp blue had replaced the dark gray clouds. When I opened the window, I breathed in the fresh air deeply, and then let out a long sigh. I looked ahead and could see glints from cars zipping by on the highway through the thick trees. I relished the thought that there were only a few more buildings to go and anxiousness about my hospital experience began to quell. I felt the warmth of my present life's energy returning the closer we came to the exit until I happened to glance over at one of the last buildings on the right. Without forethought I blurted out, "I don't like that building!"

Valerie immediately stopped the car.

"No, you don't have to stop, Valerie, I just said I don't like it, that's all."

Valerie stepped on the gas pedal with such delicate precision that allowed everyone to stare a long time at the building that I didn't like.

It was one story with a many-paned windowed wall. Through the windows was a wide hall and on the other side of the hall was another windowed wall with a courtyard in the rear where an old tree grew.

The hair on my neck rose. I knew this place all too well. I knew more than anything I was in this building before.

Debbie noticed a sign out front that read, "Nurses Training." I told her I didn't care what it said. I knew they used part of the building to perform surgeries and the other part was admittance and a visitor's center. Everyone gawked in silence.

Suddenly, I noticed the car turning and realized that Valerie was making a wide U-turn to go back into the hospital! "What are you doing Valerie?" I shouted.

"I want you to get a closer look."

"I don't want a closer look. I already know all about that building! Let's just leave."

It was an odd thing that Valerie and Debbie both played a significant role in the confirmations of my previous life and each in their own way seemed to relish their self-prescribed duties of being my investigative assistants. The problem was that they continued to negate my requests. I really wanted to leave and became more anxious. "We still have to go all the way to Bodega Bay before the sun goes down…Don't forget!" I said with assertion as if it was going to work.

There was an uncomfortable quietness in the car as my sister, undaunted, drove slowly to the back of the building. I was literally beside myself.

Several cars in the parking lot made me uncomfortable. Then she had the audacity to park! I was trying to get her to drive away and to leave this place, so I blurted out, "I thought this place gave you the creeps Valerie. Remember that sign, *Satan lives here*?"

No one said a thing. They just stared at the building and then me as if I would discover some other miracle manifestation from the great beyond.

"So, do you notice anything else?" Valerie whispered.

"No…Nothing," I stated emphatically.

"Did you do a sketch of this building?" Debbie asked.

"No…No, I didn't. So, can we leave now, please?"

Valerie finally took heed, backed out and headed towards the exit.

I breathed a sigh of relief for the second time. As we were driving towards the exit, I pondered Debbie's question, had I sketched it before. I thought it odd, in a way, that I hadn't since much of the horror happened in that building. Even though our tour through the hospital grounds verified all of my other drawings, this particular building should have been the most important for me to sketch. I quickly deduced that I hadn't because the worst of my memories took place behind those double doors.

As we neared the exit once again, I looked at the sign 'Nurses Training' and wondered if I could find out more about that building.

Valerie slowed her approach to the exit, and I joked, "Don't *even* think about doing another U-turn!"

All of us began laughing, each adding our own emphasis. I'm more than ready. We've seen enough! Yes, let's get out of here! With my hands clasped over my heart, I was the last to comment, "Thank you, Lord!"

We reached the highway and our 'tour guide' asked happily, "Now where to?"

"How about we get something to eat, it's almost noon," Rayanne suggested. "I'm hungry." Everyone agreed. Valerie quickly merged onto the highway towards town and began passing cars right and left.

Leaning forward I said to her, "Oh, so now you drive fast?"

Innocently, she quipped "What?"

As I watched the lush, green trees whiz by, I began to relax and feel my confidence slowly return. When I thought again about the window-walled building, I realized how much the sign didn't sit right with me. My creative mind that has always been able to solve problems quickly went to work. As I pondered how I could find the history of that particular building, a solution came to me. "I have an idea," I announced to my cohorts.

Debbie has been in a number of plays both acting and dancing and can be quite dramatic. Her head turned towards me so fast that her long, dark chestnut hair swung around almost hitting me in the face. She looked straight into my eyes, "Now what?"

We laughed until our sides hurt.

"You're too funny Debbie!" In strong contrast to feeling emotionally wrought yet detached while driving through the hospital, I was beginning to feel better. The trip through the hospital grounds was weird and creepy but now we were onto a different destination and I took in a deep breath. At the same time, I wanted more proof other than just driving through the hospital and verifying my memories. Suddenly, a hunch on how we might do that came to me.

I leaned forward, poking my head between the two front seats and made a suggestion, "How about this; you two can drop us off at the library and get us something to eat while we research the hospital buildings? Maybe I could find information about the building that I didn't like...you know, the one with the windowed walls?" They all said that my new plan was a great idea; especially the lunch part and then I began to think about everything that happened so far.

I found what I came looking for, verifications of what I had recalled. I think that part of me was hoping my past life was a fantastic imagination but now I had proof. However, I had no idea what was about to happen.

Dancing with Phantoms

On the way to the library as Valerie drove through the historic district, I started looking for what used to be Sarah's home. I began to feel unsettled just as I felt going through the hospital and realized that I was reluctant to find it. I just wanted to peek into my past life, not have it infiltrate my very being.

Valerie was again driving slowly, up one street and down another. As we turned a corner, I saw one large home that startled me. I don't think it was the one, but it was very similar. I was staring at it when a scene suddenly flashed in front of me. It was a memory from inside Sarah's home.

I was standing at the top of the stairwell. My grandmother lay lifeless on the landing below. Slouching over her body was a man I think was my uncle. He turns and stares into my eyes. A heavy feeling of guilt burns my face. Suddenly a terrifying scene in the hospital plays out in my mind.

I quickly shoved the memory aside and shook my head to throw off the awful feelings. Debbie looked at me.

"Are you okay?" she asked.

"Yes. I'm fine." I leaned forward to ask Valerie if we were almost to the library when I saw it on the next corner. Pulling into its parking lot was a welcomed relief.

Valerie and Rayanne agreed to pick us up in an hour. That would give Debbie and me time for research and for them to get lunch.

As the car drove off, we began walking towards the entrance through the parking lot, excited and nervous at the same time. I noticed a young woman with a large pile of books precariously balanced in her arms coming towards us. She was fumbling for her keys when, right in front of us, the whole pile of books toppled and scattered onto the pavement.

Debbie and I offered to help her pick them up.

As I reached for the first book, I was stunned! It was L. Ron Hubbard's book called Have You Lived Before This Life? This was the very book that enticed me to become a Scientologist ten years ago, almost to the day! Oh my God, this is so weird! I held the book up for Debbie to see at the same time she held up another book about reincarnation. Both of us with dropped jaws and raised eyebrows must have looked a sight. If the young woman noticed, she might have thought we disapproved of her choice in literature! She had at least ten books on the subject. We were speechless and I wasn't about to tell her what we were doing.

After we carefully situated all of the books back in her arms, she thanked us profusely for our help and we parted.

As we walked off Debbie said softly, "It's a sign."

"More like a billboard!" I laughed.

We took a few more steps.

I added, "Can you believe it?"

"It's just really weird."

I was flabbergasted. My head spun with questions that I had no answers for and no time to ponder. We were in the library and only had a short while to research the hospital buildings. I was hoping to uncover the truth about that sign, "Nurses Training".

The library was quiet with only background sounds of a few soft conversations. I saw a woman behind the information desk, gathered my courage, walked up and asked for help. "I'm doing research on the buildings at Napa State Hospital. Do you know where I might find something on that?" I prayed she didn't inquire why!

The woman tilted her head slightly up, thinking, and then suggested, "Maybe the Historical Society. They might have something."

She guided us to the area, pointed out a few books and went back to her station. While Debbie browsed, I grabbed a few books, one was quite large, and placed them on a long table near a window.

I figured that the large book, which had the history of the buildings, might give me some answers. On the first page was a first photo of the main building from a perspective of just entering the grounds. Lush trees lined the wide dirt roadway and at the end was a very gothic, four story building that looked like a castle. There was what appeared to be a tall bell tower above the entrance and on either side are round turrets. In the background were several more turrets atop side buildings. Right away, I understood why my drawing didn't match the main building we drove by today. This photo looked a lot more like the building I sketched.

I looked around to see if Debbie was near, but she was out of sight, so I went back to looking at the book. It was odd, after verifying the main building I half expected each new photo to trigger another memory. Even though they seemed familiar, none jumped out at me until I found it, the photo of the window-walled building! I just stared at it, feeling like I was in the Twilight Zone. Then I saw the caption at the bottom. It read, "Originally used for admittance and surgery." I felt like crying.

So many times, I tried to push aside the horrific memories and convince myself that I had already resolved enough of the pain and torment that I went through as Sarah. But those memories held tremendous trepidation, an unstable energy that bounced me in and out of that life repeatedly. I was dancing with phantoms and wondered what in the hell I was resurrecting.

Debbie walked up. "Find anything?" she asked, and then looked at me. "Are you all right, Kerry?"

"Read this."

"Oh, my God," Debbie said softly. "There it is. You were right!"

I could never understand how anyone questioned whether I was right about any of this and felt that I was the only one really qualified to do that. To me it was moot. However, I realized that my own need for proof helped to foster that notion. Besides that, I felt split in two on the reality of it all. Half of me wished it wasn't true and the other half had a resolute desire to uncover more truths still hidden in the past. Then I turned the pages back to the photo of the original building to show her.

"Wow! What a building. It looks like a castle." She looked straight into my eyes and declared, "Actually, it looks more like your drawing than the building we saw today!"

I raised my brows and nodded. "Creepy, isn't it?"

"This is a really weird day," she said. "What do you want to do now, look through some more books?"

I pointed to the books on the table. "I wish these books could be checked out, but they don't allow it." I thought for a moment and then said, "I got what I came for. Let's go see if Valerie is here yet. Besides, we still have our pilgrimage to Bodega Bay." We placed the books back on the shelves and headed out. As we walked outside, I noticed that more clouds had gathered and wondered if it would sprinkle again. As we passed the spot in the parking lot where that woman dropped her books about reincarnation, I cupped my hand over my mouth as if to say in secret, "I think she was a plant."

Debbie laughed. "Yes, that explains it."

I tried but couldn't wrap my head around all of the coincidences. Honestly, I felt like a marionette and that someone else had been manipulating my life. I looked up into the sky and then at my hands and feet looking for strings and smiled at my inside joke. Whoever it was, I wondered if they were giving me instructions in the guise of being my own instincts and then orchestrated synchronicity on my path. This has been the weirdest day of my life!

Just when we arrived at our agreed upon rendezvous, Valerie pulled up.

"Perfect timing," I said to her.

In Valerie's unique air of knowingness, she answered, "Of course."

The Rainbow

Our journey through the mental hospital coupled with the amazing synchronicity at the library that immediately followed was draining for each one of us, both emotionally and physically. Fortunately, a welcomed and relaxing chat over a nice lunch in a nearby park gave each of us a much-needed boost. We were now ready to embark on the second part of this unusual journey.

On the drive to the coast, Debbie and I chatted in the back some, as did Valerie and Rayanne in the front. In stark contrast to the scary and dilapidated mental hospital, we relaxed while taking in the comforting scenery.

The road to the coast—that was sometimes damp due to intermittent rain—is a meandering two-lane highway through rolling hills of grass dotted with farms, black and white cows, goats, giant eucalyptus trees, and oak trees donned with gray-green Spanish moss.

As we drove through patches of soft rain, Debbie hoped it wouldn't be raining when they reached the coast. For some reason, I stated quite matter-of-factly that it would clear up by the time we arrived. Debbie wondered why I was so sure of myself and I just shrugged my shoulders. I knew.

Our destination was the Bodega Head, the farthest out promontory in Bodega Bay. Just sixty-eight miles north of San Francisco, Bodega Bay was the setting for the 1963 Alfred Hitchcock film, *The Birds.* Valerie and Rayanne talked about the movie as they kept their eye out for large black birds.

I rolled down the car window to smell the ocean and feel the cool air on my face. I looked at my sister and smiled. Our visit to the hospital seemed to disturb her deeply and I wondered if she might have also been there in another life. I knew that she was more affected than she let on, but I had no idea why. Quickly, I let that train of thought leave. It was a bit too much.

We drove all the way out to the promontory until the road ended and then parked. Debbie and I began walking out to the point on the small trail. We were on the lookout for the rock island in the middle of the bay that her brother and sister-in-law managed to reach. As we were walking, I turned back to see where Valerie was. She and Rayanne weren't very far along and they seemed to be taking it quite slow. I yelled, "Are you coming?"

Valerie yelled back, "We'll be there."

As we walked on the narrow trail dampened by recent rain, we saw beautiful wildflowers everywhere. The wind was blowing, and the sky appeared somewhat threatening. I turned back often to see where my sister and Rayanne were and couldn't understand why they were taking so long. However, I wanted to stay with Deb and pay attention to her, so we just kept walking.

When we reached the head of the promontory where the open ocean meets the bay, Debbie pointed. "There it is. There's the rock island."

It was small, black and barren. I couldn't imagine being able to swim in those waters, especially since they are so cold. I thought it a miracle that two of them survived the accident, but I didn't want to contemplate the fate of Debbie's father.

We stared out into the bay and the waters that snatched him and stood in silence. The light began to change. I turned towards the vast ocean behind us and noticed that the sun was breaking through the clouds. When I turned back, the end of a misty double rainbow appeared right above the rock island. We both had tears in our eyes.

Just then, Valerie and Rayanne walked up. "Look," I said and then pointed to the rainbow.

Valerie said softly, "Yes, we saw it." She was crying.

"What is it?" I asked.

She sighed. "I couldn't come quickly because…"

"What?"

"Because I saw Debbie's father, under the water tangled up, stuck in seaweed. Honestly, I don't understand why I feel this way."

I spoke with certainty. "Look at the rainbow. It's a sign. He's all right now."

With the sun on our backs and wind blowing through our hair, we held onto each other and stood on the bluff overlooking the bay in awe of God and nature. The double rainbow continued to display its full spectrum of colors with its end misting onto the rock island. We watched it for several minutes more until it finally faded away. Afterwards, we gave each other long hugs and wiped our eyes. This would be a day that each of us would never forget.

The following morning, I sat on the edge of my bed. In my lap rested two books, my journal opened to the page about Sarah and the sketchbook with the images that I drew of Napa Hospital during the trip there. I reread the journal page about Sarah and then looked at my drawings.

A heavy feeling came over me. It was one thing to recollect the story and feel the terror of my past life. It was quite another to actually face that it was real. It felt *too* close and *too* real. I didn't like it, but again for some reason I couldn't leave it alone.

As I thought more about Sarah's travesties she experienced, a deep and seemingly permanent sadness draped over my soul like a heavy blanket of oppression. Funny enough, I literally pictured a blanket, which triggered a childhood memory of mine from *this* life.

We were camping and it was cold when I was trying to go to sleep. My mother put so many blankets on top of me that were so heavy I couldn't move and was still cold! I smiled at the snippet of memory; however, this blanket was quite different. The memories of that life were not anything one would be able to laugh about later. At least when I was camping, I knew I would get up in the morning, eat a hearty breakfast and explore the wilderness with family and friends. Sarah did not have that option.

Sarah's life was sitting in the forefront of my mind like a movie; scenes inside hospital rooms and Sarah's home played repeatedly, characters that were dear and characters that were pure evil, places of love and places of torture. I knew all of them.

Yes, my drawings matched, and my memories felt like a dark nightmare taking over my life. It's just too much for me to process.

Carissa quietly walked into the room. "What are you doing Mommy?" She tilted her little head. "You look sad."

"Oh, honey, I'm fine," I said.

Looking at her sweet face, I smiled reassuringly and decided to put it all away. As I was shutting the journal, a strange realization emerged; the urgency that I feel to resolve my past is coming from Sarah. I lovingly put my hand over the journal and made a promise to her. We will get through this someday. I just can't do it right now. I felt she understood and had faith in me. When I placed the books in my drawer, a feeling of calm came over me and I smiled.

I picked up my little girl and gave her a big, warm hug and kiss. "I love you so much!" I said to her. She giggled. We walked into the living room and I let go of the past knowing that someday, when the time was right, I would face it again.

As Barbara walked back into the kitchen, I was wiping my hands. "All done." I said.

"Me too."

I looked at Barbara, "Are you tearing up?"

She wiped her eyes. "A little."

"The story about Debbie's father," she began then added, "and what happened to you on that trip. I don't know what else to say."

I looked at her and said, "Makes it all the more real, doesn't it?"

She nodded, then added, "Too real."

We went back to the living room and sat down. I looked at Barbara, "You seem tired."

"I am. I don't think I slept enough last night. Would you mind if I took home some chapters to read tonight? I'm going to take a nap and then I will be all refreshed."

I looked at my chapter list and then said, "One of the chapters may be difficult to read since it is graphic. Are you okay to read that on your own?" I asked.

"I'll be fine, but if it is, I'll wait, just like you suggested."

"Okay. Are six chapters too many?"

"I'm a fast reader. That should be fine. Also, if I can't get through it all I'll save it for the next time."

I went into the other room, grabbed the chapters and her coat. "At least your coat is dry," I said.

She then placed the chapters safely in her satchel and put on her coat. Then, she looked at me and gave me a big, warm hug. "I'm so glad we met."

"Me too," I said and smiled.

When I opened the door, we were both relieved that the sun was breaking through the clouds.

"Yay, no rain," she said.

She turned around when she got to her car and I waved goodbye. As I watched her drive off, I wondered two things; I hope my writing is okay and I hope what I described isn't too disturbing for her. Then I made light of it by thinking, well at least it couldn't be as disturbing as it was for me and shook my head.

On her way home, Barbara stopped at a light. The streets dampened by the rain reflected the trees, lights and her thoughts. Kerry was so brave to go to Napa and drive through the hospital. I can't imagine how difficult that must have been. Even though she makes light of it now, I'm sure that experience was more disturbing than she lets on.

With the light green now, she softly pressed her foot down on the gas pedal and more thoughts emerged. She shook her head slightly. *It's amazing we met that day.* Her eyes looked up to the sky and the rays of light streaming down through parting clouds. *I wonder if our meeting was one of Kerry's synchronistic experiences and now, I'm in her magical world.*

Samuel

I woke slowly. Visions of my past stood point-blank in front of me. Jimmy leaving; Nan; the blessing ceremony in the vineyard; Grandmother and Dr. Simpson all seemed as though they just happened for the first time. I rubbed my eyes to help me wake up then sighed. Some memories are bittersweet.

A man was near me. At first, I was startled. Is he part of my vision? I rubbed my eyes again. No, he's still here. Then I realized he was the one who had made gestures to the sky.

I looked down at my legs and realized that the sun moved a lot and I was now in the shade. I mumbled, "I must have slept or been daydreaming a while."

My eyes fixed upon the man and wondered where the old woman visiting him was and then I remembered she had left. I couldn't help but watch his graceful dancing movements. For some strange reason he didn't scare me, even though he was a bit odd, like Patty said. As I watched this 'dance', I could make out that this time he was doing a waltz with the air or maybe an invisible person.

Then I felt sad as I thought wistfully about Jimmy. We never went to the dance. He never held me in his arms like that. However, I realized that the sadness I felt about him then seemed a world away and pale in comparison to how I was feeling today. Now, look where I am.

Waltzing brought the 'gesturing man' closer and now he was in earshot. I spoke up without thinking, "You make a nice couple." Then thought, Jimmy and I would have made a nice couple.

He actually turned and was looking right at me! I hope he isn't like Catlady! I don't think I could handle that now.

First, he seemed to be excusing himself from his dance partner, then he bent at the waist with a graceful bow having one arm out and one at the waist and responded, "Thank you my dear, and Martha thanks you too."

"Who's Martha? I asked.

"I'm sorry. Please, forgive me. She is my dance partner and I haven't even introduced you."

With that he extended his hand to the right of him where there was nothing but space and said, "Martha, I would like you to meet this nice young lady." He paused and placed his hand out, palm and index finger up. I knew that he wanted my name.

"Oh, my name is Sarah," I said.

"Yes, yes, of course. This is Sarah. Sarah, I would like you to meet Martha," he said.

His innocent demeanor and childlike behavior brought me joy and I couldn't help but smile.

"Nice to meet you," I said.

"Martha and I have been having a wonderful time out here in the sunshine. It is beautiful here, and the flowers are lovely this time of year." He turned his head and with a wide grin motioned to the garden with his hand, "I think we have the most royal garden for miles 'round, don't you?" he asked.

"Uh," I muttered. Then I turned, paying attention to where he was pointing. I noticed that the flowers seemed especially brilliant, as if I hadn't ever seen them before. They glistened, yellow, red and pink in the brightness of the sun. "Yes," I confirmed, "they *are* quite beautiful, quite."

"Do you come here often?" he asked politely.

"Um," I hesitated, wondering if he knew where we were exactly, and then I decided to go along with him, "Yes, yes, I do. I like it out *here*. Do you come here often?"

"Oh, yes, ever so much. Oh no!" he exclaimed, "I am so sorry. I forgot to introduce myself to you."

With that, he approached me, reached down and picked up my hand. He lifted it close to his mouth, but not touching his lips. "My name is Samuel. It is so very nice to make your acquaintance."

"Why, thank you," I said, almost blushing. "Gosh," I thought, he is so easy to talk to, not like Katherine at all! I nearly curtsied.

The more we talked, the more I felt transported to another realm and out of the reality of this Saturday and the recent unearthed memories and confusion. For some reason I found myself talking and talking. I felt as though I had escaped this place and was enjoying every moment of this lovely escape. Samuel was so easy to talk with. Ideas just popped in my head. Ideas I hadn't thought of before. He made me feel welcome and privileged to be part of his unique world; a world that was very much different from what I'd experienced and for the first time in a very long while, I felt safe.

After meeting Martha, I met Ben, an old friend of Samuel's, who used to drive him in a horse drawn carriage all around town. Then he introduced me to a man with a funny name, Nilakantha Sri Ram. Samuel began quoting him and used an East Indian accent to spout out sayings that I tried to understand, but they were like questions in riddles to me. I did understand that Sri Ram was a Freemason and a philosopher. He spoke of something called Akashic Records and said that they held the complete account of all human experience and of the universe!

The idea of a book containing so much information perplexed me. "Do you have that book?"

He smiled sweetly and said, "No, my little Sarah. The Akashic Records are in the etheric realm, the invisible realm of the universe, but anyone can access the records by concentrating and using their imagination. Besides, it would be far too enormous to publish!"

Samuel continued with his explanations. At first, I had many questions that he politely answered until I realized that his answers made me think of even more questions! Finally, I just listened and tried to make some sense of it all.

Samuel must have felt more comfortable with me because he sat down on the bench right next to me. He smiled at me as if he were happy to have found an old friend.

After a bit, he began talking about his many travels. He picked up a nearby stick and drew outlines in the dirt of where each place was, like a grand map of the world. First, he drew the United States, and put a dot in New York.

I piped, "That's where my friend Patty's father is now. She just showed us a postcard from the World's Fair!"

"New York *is* quite the exciting place!" he added. Then my attention went to the scratching sound of the long line he was drawing in the dirt all the way to India. "I traveled this way," he said pointing to the line, "in a big ship and then traveled on the land of India atop a great elephant called Abhi."

"Really? Oh my goodness! Does that name mean anything?" I asked.

"Why, yes," he explained. "It means *Fearless*."

"That's good because I would be frightened to ride such a large animal!"

"It is safe, really. I was in a howdah."

"How what?"

"A howdah. It is a very large saddle," he began to offer details of the large carrier, when I interrupted again.

I couldn't help myself, and asked, "Howdah your legs go over the elephant's back?" and instantly started giggling at my own joke.

At first, he didn't get it and then politely laughed with me. "You are funny, Sarah. I like that one." Then he continued his explanation, "The saddle is actually a platform that sits on top of a large colorful rug draped over the back of the elephant." Samuel began to draw the shape of the howdah in the dirt as he explained it. "On top of the platform are chairs and because it is hot in India, the chairs are covered by a canopy to shade you from the sun. In the chair behind me was a man with a feathered fan to cool me down. My howdah had long gold tassels dangling down from the roof that moved back and forth with each step the elephant took."

"I bet the tassels gave some breeze too!" I surmised.

Samuel's eyes met mine. "In fact, they did. You are very bright too, Sarah." He went on to explain that sitting on top of the head of the elephant was the Mahout who is like our cowboys. The Mahout directs the elephant's movements with a long skinny stick. Samuel smiled and said with a sigh, "It is all so very beautiful there." Then he began swaying back and forth, as if he were high atop the elephant.

"It sounds wonderful and exciting, Samuel. You must have loved it!" I exclaimed.

Samuel went on to tell me about how he met Sri Ram in India and that he went back there several times to visit him. He also became friends with others when he went to foreign places and he talked about his mode of travel in each country: in Egypt, he rode a camel, in China a rickshaw, and in Mongolia and Tibet, he rode on horses much smaller than ours!

We talked for the rest of the afternoon until the bell sounded for dinner.

I was tired from all the excitement, exhausted by drawing up visions of other worlds, and the cool evening air had given me a bit of a chill. Samuel noticed me shivering and draped his over-shirt on my shoulders.

"Thank you," I said.

Almost everyone else had gone inside and the courtyard felt as though it had another life, as if we were lifetimes away on the beautiful grounds of a grand hotel in India. Samuel picked up my hand again and brought it once more practically to his lips, pretending to kiss it ever so gently.

"A most enjoyable afternoon, Sarah. I do hope we can see each other on the morrow. The day will not bring sunshine until I see your fair face again."

I smiled and nodded. Since I was going inside, I tried to give back his shirt.

"Dear, Sarah," he said, "Keep it for tonight and I shall retrieve it when next we meet."

I thanked him again and said, "On the morrow, then." I've never used 'morrow' before, I thought. I like that word. As I watched him walk off, I thought of how different I felt in his company. Samuel treated me like an old friend, and even though it was all pretend, it seemed more real than anything did. I was excited to meet Samuel out here in our royal garden under the sun the next day, as he had hoped.

On the way to the cafeteria, I wondered why Samuel talked to me and not that old woman. I wondered why he was here. I've come to learn though, that for each person here there is a story and the only thing that is similar with each story is some form of sadness. Of this, I was sure. What was Samuel's sad story?

I decided to go in and try to eat the food. Maybe, I could imagine it being good food, like from India, New York or China, but that would be a stretch. As I got closer to the community room doors, I felt the pleasantness of my grand garden fantasy begin to fade. The closer I came, the louder the din of unpleasant sounds and voices that I had come to loathe increase. The closer I came the more the reality of this place cast a pall on my pleasant afternoon with Samuel.

I began again to fear for my own fate. As I worried about that and my future, I heard a reassuring voice in my head, *"You will be alright."* I realized that it was Patty's voice, as if she were right by my side watching out for me. However, the moment I walked through the doors; I knew that I couldn't imagine anything worse than where I found myself right at this moment. Words of assurance couldn't protect me from this inescapable reality.

Patty was at our table and motioned me to sit by her. "Where have you been?" she asked.

I didn't want to tell her anything about my bittersweet memories or my afternoon with Samuel. I didn't want her to say anything that might spoil it more. I just wanted to keep the past where it belonged and my friendship with Samuel as my own private escape, but she had no inkling of my ponderings.

"So, Sarah," she began, "Did you recall anything at all?"

God, do I have to? Patty just stared at me. Finally, after a few moments I said, "I did have some memories come back, but they weren't very clear. Maybe later perhaps?" *Now, that should do it.*

"Way to go, Sarah," she said. "First, it's a little and then more! Don't forget the reason you need to remember your uncle? Promise me, because if you do, you won't have any more treatments and you might be able to come home with me or at least visit!"

There was something enticing in her suggestion after all, and I promised her that I would try again.

Later that night, however, as I lay on my cot I tossed and turned my promise to her in my head. Should I keep it or disregard the idea? I wasn't sure if there was any benefit to me anyway. I just wanted to forget, not remember. That's all. Every time I tried to put it out of my mind, I saw Patty's face and her crescent smile telling me that everything would be all right. Besides, what would I tell her tomorrow, or rather should I say, 'on the morrow'?

I smiled for a moment thinking of Samuel and our pleasant afternoon, but Patty's plan worried me. Am I just too afraid? What if she is right and remembering my uncle will help me get out of this place? The words, 'get out of this place' echoed in my head and ushered in a feeling of hope. As I considered the possibility that her plan might work, I realized that a slight hope of leaving here was better than no hope at all, so, as I lay in bed, I finally relented. I took a deep breath and began imagining what I last remembered: the blessing party, the undiluted wine, Dr. Simpson and Nan. Before long, more and more memories arose, as if they were waiting for me to come back and join them.

The Mystery Man

Sunday, May 8, 1938

In the morning, after breakfast, I decide I want to enjoy the last day off before school commences the next day and wander out to my swing. I sense that I will soon be getting too old to enjoy this childish pleasure. It is another beautiful day with blue skies and white clouds. As I lean back on the swing and peer up at the sky, I decide that I will always love looking at the clouds no matter how old I become!

Once I reach full momentum swinging forward, I lean back and gaze up at the trees filled with leaves and blue-sky patches. When I glide back down, my feet barely graze the soft grass tickling my feet. I feel free and happy. On the next swing up, I try to see over the treetops when a car's pulling up distracts me. It's the same black car I saw the day before and it parks right in front of our house!

I jump off my swing and run into the kitchen. "Bang!" goes the screen door as it hits the kitchen table.

Before Nan can chide me, I yell, "That car is back. I think he's coming to our house. Go see, Nan. Go see!"

Nan wipes her wet hands on the embroidered apron that is just as much a part of her as her own hair. She speaks in a soft scolding, "Shush young lady, you will bother your grandmother. Now you don't want to do that do you?"

"But there is someone here," I repeat. "That black car is back again!"

"Oh, it's probably someone who wants to rent, like you thought he was," she says.

"No!" I respond earnestly. "He's coming up here. I'm sure of it. Do you suppose it's a salesman?"

Nan scoffs at my concern but makes her way to the front room while I follow close behind. When she stops in front of the large picture window, I stand beside her clutching the edge of her apron.

She tilts her head and peers out the window. "I cannot imagine who would call without prior notice," she says. "You know your grandmother does not approve of such a thing."

The man gets out of the car, brushes himself off and stands tall at the gate in his black suit. His eyes cascade our house from top to bottom and over and about the colorful grounds, as if he's familiar with all of it. He smiles queerly and hesitates some moments before opening the gate. Once entered, he stands underneath the trellised arbor, as if surveying the rose covering and then takes in a quick whiff of the scented roses. He plucks a pink bud from a rosy tendril and places it onto his lapel.

I peer up at Nan. Alarmed that he would have the presumption to pluck one of our roses for himself, "Who is he?" I whisper.

Her eyes, which seem to be getting worse all the time, still cannot make out this mysterious man. When his foot lifts to take the first step on our stairs, she gasps. "I do not believe my eyes!" she exclaims in her strong French accent.

"What, Nan? Who is that man?" I ask anxiously.

Half covering her mouth in amazement, she speaks as if talking just to herself, "I cannot believe that Joseph would show his face here again."

I can't stand the suspense any longer and yell, "Who is Joseph?"

Nan turns and without hesitation explains, "You must know, Sarah. Joseph is your one and only uncle, your grandmother's only son and your mother's only brother."

"Okay, okay, okay, I get it. But I didn't even know I had an uncle...or that my grandmother had a son or that my mother...."

"That will be enough of that. You make too much fun of me already."

I laugh aloud at her. She is very easy to make fun of, though I would never do it meanly. I love Nan.

But now a hard knocking on our front door interrupts our intimate chiding. Before I can say a word, or run to get the door, Nan puts her hand firmly on my shoulder, bends down to my ear and whispers emphatically, "I want you to not answer the door. I want you to go into the backyard and stay there until I call for you. I will go upstairs and tell your grandmother who is here, and she will know what to do. Do you understand me?"

A chill runs down my spine. Without the slightest faltering, I raced through the living room past the grandfather clock, past the basement door and pantry, into the kitchen, bolt left to go out the side door and into the backyard. There, I jump back onto my swing in perfect cadence with the banging of the screen door. But my heart is pounding. My mind races with questions. Why didn't I know about him? Why is Nan so serious? Why doesn't she want me to meet him? Why must she prevent me from seeing him right away? I suddenly feel light-headed just like I had in Church. Oh God! I hope I don't faint.

I slide off the swing and my feet plop down on the cool grass. But the trees begin to swirl round and around and no matter what, all my strength escapes me. In slow motion, as if I'm watching from afar, I collapse sideways onto the lawn. My heavy eyes open slowly. Coming into focus are two black legs. Then, I remember the man in the black suit. The bright sky blinds me as I notice my 'uncle' is staring down at me.

"Sarah? Is that you? Are you all right?" he asks.

He bends down, slips his arm under my shoulders and lifts me up. "I can't believe it, after all these years, my how you've grown. You look just like sis did when she was your age," he says. "Did I startle you? Don't be afraid. I'm your Uncle Joseph," he explains. "I'm sure you've heard of me."

He places his hand under my arm and helps me up. "Will you be all right?"

There are only two things I'm aware of: my energy has returned, and I want to get as far away from this man as I can. No longer light-headed, I bolt for the kitchen door yelling, "Nan, Nan, come here! Nan, he's here! He's out here!"

Standing behind the kitchen chair, I cling to its sides tightly. He follows me, walks in the back door calmly with an air of confidence and stops by the door. He takes off his hat and with a slight grin, nods his head as he slowly studies the room. "It hasn't changed a bit. No, it sure hasn't," he says twirling his hat in his hands.

I see Nan now, coming from the living room and I make a motion with my head that he is in here. Uncle Joseph notices my nod and watches the door to see who will enter. "Nan," he shouts, "you look the same as when I last saw you."

Uncle Joseph quickly goes over and wraps his arms around Nan's large waist. She does not return the hug and he does not even mention my fainting. "Where's mother? Is she well?" he asks then glances in the direction of Grandmother's room. "I'll just go up and see her."

Nan moves to stand in front of the doorway that leads to the front room crossing her arms in defiance. "No, Joseph, you're not to go up," she speaks in a stern voice that I would certainly obey. In order for him to pass, he'd have to move her aside and I can tell that he too, would not venture the outcome of such a move.

"Okay, okay, Nan, you win. When can I see mother? I've come a long way to do just that," he claims. Then, my new uncle casts his eyes on me, smiles and continues, "And, of course to see Sarah, and you too Nan. How could I forget you?"

Before Nan can respond I pipe up, "How far did you come from?"

"All the way from Indianapolis."

"Is that real far?" I ask.

Before Uncle Joseph can answer, Nan instructs him to go to the parlor and wait, and that Grandmother will be down to speak to him in due time. He asks if there were any brandy. Nan, in a sudden shift in priorities, instructs me to serve him from one of the snifters in Grandmother's liquor cabinet while she attends to Grandmother.

We follow Nan down the hall and into the parlor and once Nan sees that I am getting him his drink, she turns and goes up the sweeping staircase.

The parlor is by far the most magnificent room in our house. It is directly across from the living room and contains Grandmother's finest furnishings and decorations. Some she'd collected during her trips about the world and many others were treasured heirlooms. It is not often Nan or Grandmother allow me into the parlor since it is for receiving guests.

My favorite place to sit is by the leaded glass bay window—Grandmother calls it an alcove—that overlooks the street and garden. In front of the alcove are two Queen Anne style chairs. Grandmother nestled between them around a lace-covered table, decorated with a small hand painted oil lamp, an antique Chinese figurine and a Chinese vase. She always keeps freshly cut flowers from her garden in this room, one in the Chinese vase and another on our piano. On my way to get the brandy, a whiff of the flowers' sweet aroma draws me to take one deep breath of their fragrance. So lovely are the scents of roses and pine greens.

Uncle Joseph walks over to the piano and starts tapping on a few keys. "Does your grandmother still play?"

"Not very often anymore," I answer.

"Is anything wrong with her?"

I don't answer because Grandmother wouldn't like it.

He stops playing, walks over to the alcove and sits down in one of the chairs. My eyes focus on the liquor cabinet made of fine mahogany at the rear of the parlor. It stands next to the pocket doors that open to our formal dining room. I step carefully across the thick Oriental rug that Grandmother bought on a trip to the Far East years before I was born.

For some time now, I've been the one to serve our guests their drinks. It began one day when Nan was frightfully busy in the kitchen and asked me to serve our callers their choice of beverage in its proper glass. Each liquor and particular wine have its own crystal glass (of which Grandmother has every shape, style and size). She never boasts about the perfection of her crystal, but some of our guests can't help noticing. The set sparkles brightly in its own glass-enclosed cabinet. Some of the crystal is silver or gold rimmed. Others are decanter sets for aperitif or port and are colored and etched beautifully.

Grandmother instructed me thoroughly as to which liquid and why it should go into which appropriate drinking glass. This was of course only after I had made a complete blunder by serving someone brandy in a tall champagne flute. Slightly behind the cover of my long blond hair, my eyes follow Uncle Joseph as I prepare his brandy. He stands up and wanders slowly about the room picking up and fondling the antiques that I never dared touch, as if he had any business doing so. But I feel as though he were gathering lost memories. Why didn't I know about him? Did he run away long ago? Why is he here now? So many questions run through my mind that I am certain I will absolutely burst with curiosity; yet I know it's not my place to ask, at least not yet anyway.

"I'll bet you're curious about your Uncle Joseph, aren't you?" he asks abruptly.

I'm shocked that he can read my mind and I'm not sure what to say. I don't answer him, but finish pouring his brandy. Then I carry the "goldfish glass", as I call it, to him with its narrow stem and rounded snifter cleft between my index and middle finger.

"I can understand your surprise," he says, taking the brandy from my hand, "It's not every day an uncle comes into your life. From the way you," he began, and then cleared his throat while mocking my having fainted by imitation, "you first acted when I arrived." He chuckles.

"I bet you didn't even know you had an uncle, did you?" He studies me as he awaits the reaction I don't give, and then continues undeterred, "I, myself, am quite surprised to see how grown up you are!" He puts his hand on my waist giving it a little squeeze adding, "You know I haven't seen you since you were just a baby."

"Sarah, Sarah," yells Nan from the top of the stairs. I slip from Uncle Joseph's grasp and dart out of the room and up the stairs. Nan stands right in my way with her hands perched atop her hips, commandingly. I can never understand why it is acceptable for Nan to yell at me, but if I raise my voice even a trifle, she considers it unladylike. One day when Nan scolded me, I finally concluded that she must not consider herself a lady.

Nan motions for me to come with her. She begins her descent down the stairs, and I follow quietly behind through the living room, past the cellar door and into the kitchen. She asks me to get a jar of goose pate while she begins slicing the French bread just delivered this morning. Nan keeps our pantry, which sits opposite to the cellar door, stocked with Grandmother's favorite foods. I know just where the pate is—top shelf, left side.

Sometimes, when Nan asks me to get something out of the pantry, I am full of excuses. She would say that I was lazy, and I would always tell her I wasn't. I always do just about anything else she asks me, but the pantry, even though it is full of my favorite foods too, frightens me. The heavy door always shuts itself before I can pull the cord to turn on the light. Then, everything becomes black as a cave. It was in that small, dark room where once I felt the presence of some kind of monster and I couldn't get out of there fast enough! Finally, I resolved the problem. Now, I open the door, reach in, grab a nearby can and place it on the floor in the door jamb before I go in and pull the light cord, but for some reason that room still makes me uneasy.

Today however, I am a bit too distracted and excited about our mysterious guest. The pantry monster isn't worth a second thought, I determine. After propping open the door, clicking on the light, and climbing the stepladder, I grab the pate Nan requested and rush back into the kitchen.

"Did you switch off the light?" she asks knowing, full well, I hadn't.

"No-o-o," I reply. Once I do and my 'propping can' is back on its shelf, I go back to Nan's side for more instructions.

"See. That wasn't so hard now was it?" she says with a big smile. Just as usual, Nan manages to pay me back for mocking her earlier, and as usual, I pretend not to hear.

"May I arrange the bread?" I ask.

"Certainly Sarah."

Nan has set two glass platters on the counter, one for the bread and pate, and one for grapes. On one, I carefully place the bread in a circular pattern around the mound of pate while Nan washes the grapes and puts them on the other platter. On the serving cart, she lays two pink tinted glass plates, two cloth napkins, and a small but ornately wrought knife alongside the food.

"Let me take it in Nan," I beg.

"My, my, you want to do everything. What do I get to do?"

"Oh, Nan let me, please."

"You can wheel all this in through the dining room," Nan instructs. "I want you to be careful now, not to let the cart get stuck on the rugs, and I want you to come right back. I'm certain that they have some important business to discuss and this is not a time for you to listen in on adult matters."

Reluctantly I agree, even though I want so much to know more about Uncle Joseph and why he is here out of the blue all the way from Indianapolis.

Through the doorway, I can see Grandmother sitting in a corner of the alcove with her back in a perfectly upright, dignified posture. She is wearing one of her best dresses of blue lace adorned with tiny glass buttons. Uncle Joseph sits opposite her. I decide to proceed ever so slowly, not to spill of course, and if I am extra quiet I might, at the same time, be able to satisfy some of my curiosity before Grandmother asks me to leave.

They are apparently in the middle of speaking of his trip. Then, Grandmother asks how long it took and Uncle Joseph begins explaining everything in lengthy detail. I am finally in the parlor when Uncle Joseph now asks a question of Grandmother.

"How is your health?" he asks, then leans forward in his chair appearing most concerned. She ignores his question and notices that I have entered the room and am crossing it with the speed of a snail.

"My dear Sarah, you needn't go that slowly," she comments. I realize they are now aware of my presence and their conversation will certainly yield no more answers to feed my curiosity. I speed up, just a little though, in case I am wrong. Uncle Joseph comments that I am beautiful, like my mother Clara. Grandmother agrees, but I notice she remains aloof towards him even when speaking about me, which is not at all like her. I serve them their afternoon hors d'oeuvres slowly, until I receive an, 'I could take my leave' nod from Grandmother. Noting my obvious disappointment, she gives me a reassuring smile. I know that means she will let me know later what is going on, but I wonder if she will let me know everything.

Just before I reach the kitchen, I purposely step out of their line of vision and listen intently.

Grandmother asks if he is going to stay for dinner, as if that would be the extent of his surprise visit. He says he would love to, but adds quickly he hoped to stay a few days, explaining that he has come such a long way just to see her. I peek around the door and see him lean forward in his chair, resting his elbows on his knees. He continues on about how important this visit is to him and how he wants to get to know me. He takes out a handkerchief and wipes his eyes and then bows his head like a kid in trouble.

Grandmother doesn't say a thing for the longest time, and I think that maybe they became aware of my eavesdropping until I hear her finally agree to his request.

I realize that Nan might soon notice my absence and I quietly slip back into the kitchen. She has one of her hands inside a large chicken, pulling out guts, getting it ready for roasting, making me laugh out loud.

"What are you laughing at?" she asks.

"Did you get your hand caught in there, Nan?"

She just glares at me and then we both laugh.

"What do you suppose Uncle Joseph is doing here anyway Nan?" I ask.

"I don't know my dear, but whatever it is I certainly hope he finds it and then goes on his way." I can tell from Nan's tone that she is not going to tell me anything else and I decide that finding out the truth about Uncle Joseph will be something I have to do on my own.

Uncle Joseph

All afternoon Nan and I prepare dinner for our unexpected guest. Not that I had to help, I just like working with Nan and watching her cook. As she fixes her special stuffing for the chicken, I peel the potatoes and carrots and place them into cold salted water. Once we prepare everything and the chicken is roasting, Nan suggests I go outside and play before I have to get ready for dinner.

I go out of the kitchen and walk into the front yard instead of running this time. The long Summer day is still full of sunshine, but an evening breeze begins swirling through the trees this time of year cooling our river town. I look at Jimmy's house and realize how much I miss him. I wish we could talk, and I could tell him all about my uncle.

I walk around and carefully inspect the front yard. We have a tree that the hummingbirds like. I look just in time to see one fluttering and prodding its long, probing beak into a red blossom. They are in such a hurry. I always hoped that one would hold still so my eyes can catch their bright green and pink colors longer than a nibble of a second.

I go back to my swing and begin slowly pumping and pulling back until I am high up and catch a glimpse into the parlor through the tall, arching side window while swinging forward, and then I plunge down to see the kitchen as I swing back. I can see Nan by the stove and on my next return I yell, "Hi, Nan." I pull hard on the ropes leaning all the way back, pointing my toes out straight to propel me forward as I peek into the parlor. This time I see that Uncle Joseph and

Grandmother are not there. On my return back towards earth, I see Nan in the kitchen and again I yell, "Hi," After three or four shout-outs to Nan, she appears at the back door wiping her hands on her apron.

"What is it?" she asks a bit miffed.

"I was just saying 'Hi', that's all."

"It's not 'Hi', young lady, it's 'Hello' and anyway I think it's about time for you to come in, clean and change for dinner." Then she says, "I thought you might like to choose the wine." She starts to go back into the kitchen then turns back to me. "That is, of course, if I don't continue to be interrupted and dinner is never served."

I get the message and hop off my swing.

Nan prepares the room next to mine, which is down the hall from Grandmother's, for Uncle Joseph. Apparently, both Grandmother and Uncle Joseph were resting before dinner. I clean up and put on my favorite light blue dress with the shoes that match. It seems even smaller than the last time I put it on. I sigh thinking how I can't wait until August when we will make our annual trip to the city for my school and dress clothes. I take one last glimpse into my dresser mirror before I go to help Nan.

Nan is setting the table and I help her finish, all the while thinking about which wine I will pick. I am just about to go into the cellar when Uncle Joseph comes down the stairs dressed in a different suit.

"Where are you off to?" he asks.

"I'm picking out the wine for our dinner."

"Can I come with you?"

"Sure," I reply.

I purposely walk down the steps slowly, one by one, for Uncle Joseph who is right behind me. I wouldn't want him to fall! The steps are steep and close together and Nan had a tumble once, although she still brings down her pies when I'm not around and Grandmother hasn't been down here recently since she hurt her knee.

"Why are you going down the stairs so slowly, Sarah? We'll never get there," he says in mock complaint.

I glance back at him, grin, and then leap over the last four steps landing firmly on the basement cement floor. "Is that fast enough for you?"

Uncle Joseph bounds down the stairs landing right beside me. "Be careful young lady, you'll break your neck."

I switch on another light that illuminates our many tall racks filled with wine bottles. Uncle Joseph's eyes open wide. "Boy, mother has accumulated a lot more wine since the last time I was here!"

Our cellar is as big as the first floor of our house, except the ceiling is not as high. On one wall—near the steps to the side-yard by my swing—is one of our many wine racks. It stands about six feet tall and eight feet wide. In total, we stock around three hundred bottles. One rack in the back has very old wines from France.

Uncle Joseph notices a bottle with a torn piece of red material tied around its neck. "I remember these!" he says, picking one up. "Are these still the ones not to choose for dinner?"

"Yes. Those are for special occasions only." I take the bottle out of his hands and put it back on the rack. "I didn't think you would know about that."

"Well, Sarah, I used to pick out wine too when I was your age."

It seems odd to me that someone else knows about the red material. I study Uncle Joseph as he peruses the racks of wines. He has a look about him, as if he is remembering his past, but when he picks up a different bottle throated in red cloth, I get nervous and reach for the bottle.

He swiftly pulls it away from my grasp and says, "Hey, isn't the fact that I am here having dinner special enough?" looking at me as though I should agree. Nan or Grandmother, however, never before allowed me to make that choice. "Well? Shall we?"

"I don't think so. Maybe we should ask Nan."

"I thought they left choosing the wine up to you." He looks straight at me making me feel a bit uncomfortable and puts the wine back carefully. "I wouldn't want you to get into trouble. Boy, do I know what that's like!"

Feeling relieved I go back to my search. I begin carefully picking up one bottle after another, reading each label then replacing them having turned the bottles slightly, while Uncle Joseph watches my every move.

"Do you know about each of these wines?" he asks.

As I continue to turn the bottles, I answer, "Mostly." I think about dinner and what wines would go well. After checking twenty or so bottles I ask, "Did you know Grandmother's grapes made most of the wine on these racks?"

"No, I didn't Sarah." He notices the bottle of zinfandel I'm considering. "I'm impressed. You seem to know a lot about wines. Where did you learn all this from?"

"Oh, Grandmother mostly, but Mr. Peabody taught me quite a bit about how wines are made and the difference between a good wine, a bad wine and an excellent wine."

He curls his brow and asks, "Who is this Mr. Peabody?"

"He was a dear friend of Grandmother's and mine."

"Isn't he a friend anymore?"

"No, it's not like that. He, well, he died last year, and this will be the first year that I haven't gone with him to watch the grape harvest." My head tilts down. I think about how much I miss Mr. Peabody.

"I'm sorry," he says, "It must be difficult for you and Grandmother. But hey, maybe I could take you to see the harvesting."

"Will you still be here?" I ask.

"Possibly. I hope to, at least," he says. "But you really impress me, Sarah, about how much you know regarding the business and the vineyards. It's a lot different from the shoe business and I've forgotten so much since I haven't been here in a very long time. Tell me Sarah, what else do you know about these wines?"

I feel flattered. He talks to me more like an adult, not a child of eleven. I notice that my feelings for him are beginning to change slightly from our first meeting. Maybe, I judged him too quickly. Maybe Nan was wrong. Maybe he isn't so bad after all or maybe he's changed. People can change, Grandmother always tells me that.

I begin to explain to Uncle Joseph everything I know about the making of wine, from all the different kinds of grapes to the importance of weather. I tell him how the weather has been good to us these past few years and explain that Grandmother sells her grapes to the different resorts and wineries, and that new wineries are beginning to open up everywhere.

Uncle Joseph says that he recalled that his father had sold most of the land to get by at the beginning of the Depression. I explain to him that he had, but not all of it. Since Grandfather died seven years ago and Grandmother took over the business, she managed to buy more land each year at good prices, especially since the end of prohibition. I also told him, as if it was a secret, that I believe she couldn't have done it without Mr. Peabody's help.

"How much land does Grandmother have now?" he asks.

"I don't remember. I'll ask her at dinner."

"No, no, that's not necessary," he responds quickly. "Really, it's none of my business. Tell me more Sarah. I want to know everything you know about wines and grapes, but I suppose that would take a very long time." Uncle Joseph smiles.

Half-joking, I say, "Oh that would take way too long!" I smile back and notice for the first time that his eyes are blue just like mine and he has a very pleasant face. There seems to be something special and exciting about him. I feel like I am important to him and realize for the first time that I am the one answering questions for an adult, not the other way around.

Uncle Joseph cups my chin in his hand, "Let me get a good look at you, Sarah. You really do look like your beautiful mother."

Feeling a bit uncomfortable by his grasp, I step away from him. "What was she like?" I ask while searching for that bottle again.

At first, his face takes on a distant, yet intense demeanor and then softens. "She was pleasant and thoughtful. She was quiet," he stops and looks straight at me, "I think you have part of her in you. But you have a lot of your father in you too."

"Grandmother never speaks of my parents. I think it's difficult for her." I thought about that a moment and then I riddled him with questions. "Can you tell me about my father? Did you know him well? How was I like him?"

"So many questions! Yes, I knew him very well. We weren't just brothers; we were also friends. We did a lot of fun things together." He stops talking, turns towards me, tilting his head slightly. "You are like him in that he was very mature for his age. He always knew exactly what he wanted. He wasn't just going to be anybody; he stood out and was a very independent man."

Uncle Joseph took in a deep breath and added, "He was clever too, just like you."

His comment embarrasses me a bit, but at the same time, I feel recognized for what I do know.

His demeanor relaxes and as his eyes peruse the basement, he smiles. "I used to love coming down here too, Sarah." He touches one of the cloth ties on a bottle next to him and rubs the material between his fingers as he speaks. "Sometimes, mother would let me pick the wine but only when father was out of town."

I pull out a bottle of Pinot and ask, "How about this one?" Before he can answer, I hear Nan's familiar voice calling us to come up for dinner. I grab my pick of wine and hand it to him.

He gives me an approving smile and says, "We better go up!"

When I begin to ascend the stairs, he gently holds my arm, stopping me, and asks, "Sarah, let's keep our conversation about your mother and father a secret just between us. Okay? I wouldn't want to upset your grandmother."

I push his hand off my arm, nod and bound up the stairs. When I reach the top, I turn and see that he is still at the bottom of the stairs, looking around as if he is recalling memories again.

"Uncle Joseph!" I yell. "Nan called us, remember."

Before I can turn to leave, he bounds up the stairs so quickly that he is right behind me!

"What's taken you so long, Sarah?" he jokes.

Our dinner is wonderful. Grandmother praises me for helping Nan prepare. She also mentions that I am a great help around the house. I tell Grandmother about Joseph being with me in the cellar and that I told him about wine and wine making. He mentions to Grandmother how impressed he is with all that I know and that he looks forward to learning more.

The more we talk the more I begin to notice that Grandmother doesn't seem so secretive, and that she is changing her attitude, as I had, towards Uncle Joseph. She asks him about his life at home and if he is married.

"Quite so," he answers. "I might add that I have two lovely children holding down the fort until my return."

"You mean I have cousins. What are their names?" I ask.

"Yes, you have two cousins, Sarah, and an Aunt Elizabeth."

"But what are their names? How old are they?"

"Joan is three and Ted is five."

Grandmother seems as pleased as I am to find out that we have more family than we ever knew about. We both urge him to tell us all about them, and he quickly brings out a photo from his wallet.

Joan looks like I did at her age, except she has her mother's dark hair. Grandmother comments on how much Ted looks like Joseph.

"Could I visit them sometime?"

"Sure," he says.

"That would be a long trip, Sarah," interjects Grandmother.

"Maybe they could come and visit us? That would be okay, wouldn't it be Grandmother?"

Her facial mannerism tells me that I have said too much. Uncle Joseph, who is sitting across from me, turns his head away from Grandmother and gives me a quick wink, as if to say that I am not to worry.

He picks up his napkin, carefully wipes the corners of his mouth and says, "Actually, I've been thinking about moving my family out here."

"That would be great!" I shout. Grandmother abruptly lifts her hand, addressing my lack of decorum.

"It's not as easy as all that, Sarah," he begins. "I was forced to sell my shoe business because of the Depression, and I'll have to find work and save enough money for a house before I can afford to move my family out here." He lowers his eyes and continues explaining, "Elizabeth has had to move into her parent's house until I get back on my feet."

"Grandmother, I know..." I blurt out. "Can Uncle Joseph help with managing the vineyards? You just told me last week that Roberto had too much work for one man."

Grandmother appears thoughtful, uncertain.

"Who is Roberto?" asks Uncle Joseph.

"He manages the vineyards and has been with us a long time, but since Mr. Gregorio, his assistant, passed on recently Roberto has had too much work for one man," she tells him.

"I didn't come here expecting a handout and I hadn't planned on telling you my problems, but maybe you could try me out for a few weeks and see how I do? From all I've learned today," he pauses, turns to me and then back to Grandmother, "it sounds like an interesting and challenging business and I do like a challenge. If it doesn't work out, I'm sure I can find work in my own field. I was planning on going to San Francisco because of its garment industry. That was my forte before I sold shoes. With that business just lately picking up again, I'm almost certain that I can find a sales position in the district."

Uncle Joseph and I quietly finish our dinner and await Grandmother's word. We sit in silence for a full five minutes except for the sounds of glasses tinkling, and bright silverware tapping against the Wedgewood plates as we continued to dine.

In the meantime, Nan comes in to refill the wine glasses (adding water to mine-again) and somehow manages at the same time to fill the room with a feeling of heavy disapproval.

I see Grandmother taking all this in, and I really don't think she will go ahead with our request.

"Okay, Joseph, you'll have your try at this position on one condition," she announces. He lifts his head, intently. "That if, after a month, I find that you're not cut out for this kind of work you go straight to San Francisco as you've already planned. I don't want to be responsible for your family waiting longer than they need to."

Grandmother settled it. Once she speaks, it's law. I smiled and even Grandmother ever so subtly raised the corners of her lips.

Uncle Joseph grinned handsomely and raised his glass for a toast.

"By the way, I almost forgot to tell you, Sarah picked out a perfect wine for this lovely meal."

Grandmother nodded in agreement and we all raised our glasses. Uncle Joseph began to speak, but Grandmother intervened.

"Here's to a new future for us all," she predicted.

We clicked our glasses in the table's center and sipped our wine. I thought about all the help I could give him in the next month and hoped he would stay on through summer, when I wasn't at school so I could show him more of what I know about the vineyards.

His eyes turned mischievous. "I have a great idea. First, let me ask you. Does the assistant get one or two days off—or none—on the weekend coming up?"

Grandmother, donning her perfect posture and aristocratic manners asks, "Why Joseph, what do you have in mind?"

"I was just thinking that I would love to see San Francisco. We could all make a trip of it; we might buy Sarah her new school clothes. You still go to San Francisco for school clothes, don't you mother?" She nods. "Well, why don't we go shopping? I know quite a bit about the latest fashions. In fact, I just got back from a trip to New York, looking for work, and had the chance to see some very swanky new lines. How about it, Annabelle?" he asks, addressing Grandmother by name, to my surprise.

"You seem to forget that school is almost out for the year. We won't be buying new clothes until August," she explains.

I pipe up quickly, "Yes, but my clothes are getting too small as of late."

"Do you not remember we just went to San Francisco?"

I realize in that moment that I do not want anyone to remind me about the dress that I'd probably never wear and so I glare at Grandmother, as if to say don't mention my new dress.

Uncle Joseph interrupts, "Hey, I didn't mean to start any arguments! What if we just go there and look around. We could window shop. That way we can see the latest fashions and plan our next shopping trip. How's that sound?"

After a long pause, Grandmother agrees on the trip and indicates we could go once school is out. Uncle Joseph also mentions that if she isn't happy with his work, he would be able to check on the job scene while we were there, killing two birds with one stone, as he says. He suggests we take his car, but Grandmother doesn't like that idea and politely replies, "No thank you Joseph, we'll take my car."

When I finally go to bed that night, I am so thrilled I can hardly get to sleep. Everything in my life seems to have changed in a way I never imagined and in just one day. Finding out I have an uncle, and that there is still this big mystery surrounding him, makes me think about my own parents. Sometimes, I used to feel like I never had any parents, that maybe Grandmother adopted me. Now having an uncle changes everything.

Grandmother had told me that my Grandfather destroyed all of the photos of my parents because he was so sad, and the pictures only reminded him of the tragedy. That's why I imagined I had no parents, but now I have an uncle and that changes everything! He even said that I looked like my mother! Despite what Nan suggests, I am grateful for my Uncle Joseph. He makes me feel like I truly belong.

Without warning, I begin to cry. I feel happy yet confused. I have so many questions, yet I don't know where to begin to ask for answers. There is a tap at my door. Uncle Joseph enters and sits on the side of my bed. I feel so embarrassed about crying in front of him, that I quickly wipe my eyes and stop. He asks me if everything is all right and wonders if he made me sad by coming back.

"No, I just have something in my eye. I'm glad you're here, very glad."

He strokes my hair away from my eyes, gets out his handkerchief and says, "Here, let me help. Is it your parents you're thinking of?"

"How, how did you know?"

"Well, a little angel told me."

I giggle as he leans down, kisses my forehead and speaks softly, "Just let me know if you need anything. I'm glad I lost my job even if it only means that I can be here beside you when you need someone. Remember, you don't have to feel alone anymore."

Something in his voice gives me a feeling of being secure and excited about my life ahead. Uncle Joseph stands up and reminds me of our upcoming trip to San Francisco. We both smile and he blows me a kiss as he leaves my bedroom.

My tears have stopped, and I am able to forget my questions and confusions for the night. A warm, soft breeze comes in through my open window and I turn to view a few bright stars in the night sky and catch a flicker of a falling star. Squeezing my eyes shut tight, and holding my arms folded to my heart, I make a wish that no matter what, my uncle can stay.

Window Shop

June 1938

Going to San Francisco is always exciting for me. I love getting dressed up, wearing a hat and gloves, but today is different—I am going with Grandmother and Uncle Joseph. This is going to be great. He'll know the latest fashions from New York, and he said he was certain he could persuade Grandmother into buying at least one outfit.

By the time I am ready and go downstairs, Uncle Joseph is wearing his best suit and having coffee in the kitchen. "You look beautiful," he says as I walk into the kitchen.

"Thank you, Uncle Joseph, but this dress is too small for me," I explain, tugging on the sleeves.

"Yes, you are becoming a tall young lady. I think you've even grown since I've been here," he says humorously, with a perplexed look on his face.

"Oh, you're silly. I have not."

"Is Mother up yet?"

"Yes, she'll be down shortly. It takes her a little longer to do things lately, but she is still as strong-minded as ever." We both nod in agreement.

A trip to the city is always exciting for me. As we approach the top of the hill, before the tunnel and the spectacular view of the city, the fog seems to melt away swiftly, spreading across the road as if we're dancing over clouds. When we come to the long tunnel, just before the Golden Gate Bridge, I make Uncle Joseph honk the horn—several times despite Grandmother's objection.

Then, the most beautiful sight in the world: the massively tall orange towers that stand straight up in the air suspended over our passage. I read on a building that the bridge had a dangerous history and that many brave men lost their lives who'd helped construct it. I imagine walking up the gigantic cable and envisioning its sweeping view—no matter how dangerous it might be.

As I look to my right out to sea, I notice a big white fog bank hovering like whipped cream.

Only in San Francisco can the clouds kiss the ocean. It's as if God is hugging the earth. I'd only been on the bridge a few times since it opened last year and each time it is just like the first—simply magical!

Grandmother nudges me to look to my left at the City of San Francisco sparkling in the morning light. There are many boats on the water. We have a clear view of the island where the prison walls of Alcatraz rise heavily. "Look!" I yell. "There's Alcatraz."

Uncle Joseph pipes up, "You know what happened there a few weeks ago?"

"What? What happened?" I ask.

"Three inmates that were in the woodworking shop attacked a correctional officer with a hammer."

"How awful."

Grandmother attempts to intervene. "Joseph. That is not a very pleasant subject for conversation."

"But what did they do to them?" I ask.

He smiles and appears excited to tell me. "Another officer shot two of them, one died and the two received life sentences."

"That's good," I say. "It's supposed to be for the worst criminals, isn't it?"

"Yes, but they were not very smart to be caught in the first place, if you ask me," he says.

Grandmother gives each of us a 'drop the subject immediately' look and we abide by her 'request'.

My attention turns to the city. It looks enchanting, like some place in a fairy tale. I always feel that San Francisco is magical and imagine that the fog brings the magic in from the sea.

Uncle Joseph shifts to talking about our 'window shopping' excursion and manages to convince Grandmother that she should at least let me try on some clothes, so we know what looks good on me. She actually agrees! Maybe there is magic here!

Every shop we go to, Uncle Joseph impresses us with how much he knows about clothes, and fabric, including just what styles to ask for, what I should try on, what I should disregard and all the proper accessories to match whichever apparel seems appropriate on me.

I model each outfit for them and take pleasure in the generous appraisal of my two judges as they have me turn around before them. Yet what delights me most is that Grandmother seems to agree with Uncle Joseph about his ideas for mixing and matching skirts and blouses. Rather than my trying on dress after dress to her usual marked disapproval, she actually buys me several of these items that when mixed create variations of more than one or two outfits. I have never had so much fun shopping for school clothes! And, moreover, for the first time in my memory, Grandmother genuinely appreciates shopping for me, especially since these clever combinations are both fashionable and thrifty.

Uncle Joseph is quite the salesman. I'm sure the shopkeepers, who know Grandmother and me from previous shopping trips, enjoy the imposition of his knowledge of cut and style as well as his business-like manner. Also, Grandmother has relinquished her role somewhat, giving over to my uncle's superior eye for style when it comes to me. Of course, she has always been the one to choose what I should wear. It's rare that she takes advice from anyone else, including the shopkeepers. Yet his expertise seems to have challenged all that.

On the ride home, images of the day curl over in my mind. In all, we visited three dress shops, a coat shop, two shoe stores, a millinery and a glove and leather shop and completed our journey with a delicious meal at Fisherman's Wharf. As always, we are bringing home the sourdough French bread and fresh crab to cook and feast on the next day. With the boxes of my new outfits piled up next to me in the backseat, and the smell of crab and lemon wafting from inside the trunk, I doze off having pleasant thoughts of the day and feel blessed that my uncle came into our lives.

In the beginning of his second month on the job assisting Roberto, and, as with his acumen at clothes shopping, Uncle Joseph continues to impress everyone about how much he seems to know. One day, when Roberto is busy, I get to introduce him to some of the workers and show my uncle the rest of the operation. He acts as though he is learning everything for the first time yet makes comments only a knowledgeable person can possibly express. I didn't solve this mystery until late one night.

I get up with the intention to get a snack and notice Uncle Joseph in the library studying Grandmother's books on the business. I wonder if he learned all about the business by just reading or maybe he studied hard before he came. I'm not certain either way. Then I think about what he said the first day he arrived, that he used to choose the wine just as I do now. I don't know why I didn't think of this before! He must have worked with Grandfather and it is all coming back to him now.

As the weeks pass. I watch him begin to suggest changes to Grandmother's policies, changes that Roberto previously suggested, but Grandmother never before agreed to. I don't know how he does it, but he manages to make her feel that she is the one creating these new concepts and she is the one that saved expenses and created more profit.

Nan, on the other hand, still does not take kindly to Uncle Joseph. Anytime she smirks or makes a derogatory comment about him, I become curious as to why she can't see him in the way that Grandmother and I do. When I ask her, it quickly becomes a taboo subject.

After about a month and a half, he melds into the daily routine of our lives. We go practically everywhere together. I introduce him to all the storekeepers in town that I know. Right off, he tells just about everyone how knowledgeable I am about the business, how clever I am—which I like—and what a great help I am to him.

For the first time in my life, I feel important and needed as a young adult. He treats me with respect, not as a child. Being in company with him turns into a relationship that seems more than an uncle and his niece. We have become close friends, confiding in each other on a daily basis. He never scoffs at my worries or treats them as if they were silly or childish.

I can see that Grandmother feels more confident in him too. As the profits increase, the more she realizes that he is a great asset. Quite often, she invites him into the library, where she has her office, to discuss plans and ask his opinions. Several times, I even saw her place her hand on his shoulder and smile, a gesture rarely seen.

One Sunday evening, Nan prepares us a lovely meal of rib roast with glazed potatoes, carrots and a large salad. After placing it on the side table, she tells me to let Grandmother know that dinner is ready. When I go to the library door, I can hear both Grandmother and Uncle Joseph laughing. I knock, mention dinner, and she says that they will be right there.

I sit down and while I wait, I salivate over the steaming food wishing they would hurry up. As soon as Grandmother walks out of the library she calls out, "Sarah, would you please pick out a special wine for this meal?"

"But I already did," I say.

"No, Sarah. This is a very special occasion."

I look over at her and she is smiling beatifically. I observe Joseph and he is smiling too. I know something important is up, important enough for a bottle with the red cloth tied around the bottleneck! I nod and hurry down into the basement to the rack of French wines. I already know what wine I will choose—French Bordeaux—for the meal.

When I return with the liquid treasure, Grandmother nods and Uncle Joseph does the honors of opening it up, tying a napkin around the throat and pouring. When he finishes, he picks up the water pitcher and adds water to my glass. After this he looks right at me, raises his eyebrows slightly, and then looks back at my glass. I realize that he only splashed a few drops of water in it!

He whispers, "This is too fine a wine to dilute."

We are poised awaiting Grandmother's evening ritual of a blessing and toast. She bows her head, and we bow ours. After the blessing, she stands up with her wine glass in hand, walks up to Uncle Joseph and places her hand on his shoulder. "I have made a decision," she announces. "Here's to Joseph's permanent position. I have decided that he can stay on."

Immediately, I jump up and give him a hug nearly spilling his wine, then run over and embrace Grandmother too. "Now dear," she says, smiling lightly, "we must complete the toast before you spill all of the wine."

Just after our glasses clink, I want to rush into the kitchen to tell Nan the news, but Grandmother begins discussing what this decision means for all of us. Besides, I knew she would think it improper for me to leave the table, so I must wait.

Since he has a good position now, I quickly suggest that he bring his family out right away as I am anxious to meet my new cousins before school starts. However, my idea does not prove to be a very good one.

They both agree that he needs a place of his own first and given that the harvest will be in just a few months, he will be too busy to find a proper home and also take time off to travel to Indianapolis and collect his family.

I am perplexed with Grandmother and plead, "But why can't they stay here? There's plenty of room."

"We've already discussed it Sarah."

"Besides Sarah," Uncle Joseph interjects. "You seem to forget that all the fun times we have had together these past few weeks will not be possible when my family arrives. Not that I'm planning to abandon you, it's just that I will have a lot to do and time I'll need to devote to my wife and children."

"But I can help," I insist.

"Maybe I'm being selfish," he says. "But I want to make up for lost time. I want to get to know you as if we'd never been apart." He reaches out and then clasps my hand.

"Okay," I answer softly. I knew then what he meant, though. Uncle Joseph had become like the father I never had. Our special times together would not happen nearly as often when I would be sharing him with his own children and wife. Yet, I don't quite feel right about being the cause of his not wanting his family here at this point, even though I am desperate to hold on to the warmth of this father figure.

As our dinner continues, I become thoughtful and consider that ever since the first night when he came into my room, when I was crying, he had made it a nightly routine to visit me before I went to sleep. We'd talk about the day and he'd give me a kiss goodnight. Although I am anxious to meet my aunt and cousins, his visits to my room are a special time that will end when his family arrives. I realize that I should cherish the special moments we have now. Then, I think about how much his family must miss him, like I would, so I decide that when they arrive, I will do everything I can to make them feel welcome and a part of my life.

Patty's Mother

As I sat with Patty in the community room, I felt obligated to tell her that I remembered my uncle, but for a reason I couldn't explain, it was more a feeling and I still didn't want to. She had to ask though.

"So, Sarah, is there anything you recalled?"

My brain felt foggy…I hoped she wouldn't pursue this.

"You know," she began, "your uncle. Did you remember anything?"

Even though I didn't want to answer, the images of him, how he suddenly became a part of our lives, flashed like a motion picture in my mind. I knew Patty wouldn't give up her pursuit until she'd had an answer. Perhaps, a diversion was in order, so I began scanning the room for one.

As expected, Mutt and Jeff still hadn't moved one chess piece. Catlady was nowhere in sight. Ratlady must have been off tending to her rats. Then, I glanced out of the window into the garden and spotted Samuel. He was in the midst of acting out conversations with his invisible characters. He had the sweetest smile; he made me chuckle.

"Why are you laughing?" asked Patty. She scanned the almost vacant room, and said abruptly, "You're not turning into one of *those* patients, are you? I leave you for just one night and look at what happens."

"No—no, don't worry. I'm just looking at Samuel. He's so fascinating."

"Who?"

"Samuel," I said pointing outside.

"Oh, him. How did you find out his name anyway?"

"I met him yesterday. He's actually really nice."

"Yeah, and a bit odd, like I said before," she said shaking her head.

"I think you'd like him. He's funny and he makes me laugh."

"Oh, so now he's funnier than I am. I don't know if I will like him."

"I didn't mean that. You're the funniest, I promise."

She bows from my flattery. "You're funny too, Sarah, and I don't mean that in a *crazy* sort of way. We make a good team, you and I!"

"Boy Patty, you are the only one I know that can make light of being in a mental hospital." I smiled.

As Patty watched him, I hoped my diversion was starting to work. She studied his movements then said, "Why does he talk to you? He doesn't even talk to that woman who comes to see him. In fact, I've never seen him talk directly to anyone before."

"No one?"

"Nope."

"I don't know. He's different, but I like him. Can you guess what he told me?" She didn't answer so I just continued. "He told me all about his travels all around the world and even riding an elephant!"

Patty mumbled, "Sure. Sure, he did."

I realized that her mind was elsewhere, and she didn't hear a word I said. "Did you hear me, an elephant?"

"I've been doing a lot of thinking," she said.

Her mood was now serious, and I had a distinct sinking feeling. I quickly implored her, "Let's go outside and talk with Samuel. You'll like him, really."

"What?"

"Samuel. I told you about him. We're supposed to talk today." I started to get up to go outside, but she gently held my arm until I relinquished.

She began patting my hand, just as Nan used to do to comfort me, yet her expression was one of deep sorrow. "We'll figure it out, Sarah. I know we will."

"I don't want to figure it out. What's the use anyway, Patty? I'm never going to get out of here, not like you. You have someone that wants you. You get postcards and letters and I don't get anything. I don't have anyone, at least, that I care to have."

"You have me," she said with her half-moon smile.

"I know, but you'll be gone someday, you said so."

"You will too, Sarah. I'll talk to my dad; he can do something."

I held in tears and stared at Patty squarely in the eyes. "Do you really think what *you* say is going to make a bit of difference—In here?" I held out my hands, palms up and scanned the room.

She sighed. "I don't know, Sarah. Maybe you're right, but maybe you're wrong. We at least have to try; that's what my mom said." Just then, Patty put her hand over her mouth when those words slipped out.

She mentioned once that her mother had shock treatments, but she hadn't spoken of her since. I looked at her for an explanation.

However, Patty fell silent. She glanced up, then down, then at me, and then up again. As soon tiny tears begin to run down her cheek. I placed my hand on hers.

She wiped the tears away. "It's okay. I guess I can tell you." She hesitated and then in a pleading way said, "You'll believe me, won't you?"

I squeezed her hand. "Yes, yes, of course I will Patty,"

"I wasn't going to, that is, tell you, well, because, oh, I don't know. It's just really hard to talk about." She squeezed my hand back. "But you're different Sarah. You're not like all the others. You'll understand."

I didn't have any idea about what she was trying to tell me. She hadn't talked much about her mother, just her father. I was afraid to ask because she always appeared sad when the subject came up.

Patty's words became soft and hesitant. "Have I…ever told you about my mother?"

I shook my head.

"Well, I think it's time I tell you…she wants me to."

"I don't understand."

"Don't worry, you will. At least I hope you will."

"My mother," she began with a sudden look of joy about her, "was such a wonderful and loving person. She was full of life and really cared about other people, too much really."

"Why, what do you mean, 'too much'?"

"This is hard to explain," she began. "I told you—I don't know if you remember—that my mother had shock treatments. Well, she was here before me." With that, her mood shifted. She clenched her fists on her lap, bent her head down and began to tear up again.

"It's okay Patty. You don't have to say anything, really"

"No, I do. I *have* to." Patty wiped her tears away and took a deep breath. "My mother was always different," she began proudly, "she was actually very psychic. She could predict the future."

"Are you joking?"

"No, really," Patty confirmed. "It happened all the time. For instance, one day she told me to be careful on campus because there was going to be a fight at school, and sure enough it happened. If one of my friends was going to be sick, she would tell me not to visit them, and of course, they would turn up with an illness. I took it for granted that she could tell these things and thought all mothers were like her, but now I know they aren't."

"I've heard about people like that; that's great, so interesting."

"No, no it's not. Even though she could tell these things about other people, she didn't share how it made *her* feel. One day my dad came to me and said that Mother would have to go away to a hospital for a little while, that she wasn't feeling well, that she needed to rest."

"I'm sorry, Patty. No one should have to come to a place like this."

She gave me a soft, ironic smile. "I told him that she was fine, but he had already brought her here. You see," Patty said to me quietly, "we didn't have much money because of the Depression, and this was the only place that we could afford. I didn't know until later what really happened."

"How did you find out?"

"My mother left me a journal, so I'd understand. It had a red cover made out of leather. In it, she kept notes of her visions, as she called them, and her predictions of things to come. She wrote that I should have the book, after…after she died."

Patty stopped talking for a few minutes. I didn't know what to say so I waited, distracting myself by turning slightly to watch Samuel's antics out in the yard until she spoke up again.

"After my mother came here, she seemed better for a while. She came home after a few months. She was quiet though, and I had to help her do things while my dad worked."

"You helped her just like you've helped me?"

"Yes, just like that. She'd had many shock treatments and it took her a long time to get her strength back. She seemed angry and upset about not being able to remember things. I had to help her remember. Then strange events began to take place."

Patty gathered her thoughts, built up courage to go on. I didn't know if I should say anything, so I didn't.

She finally asked, "Remember I said she was psychic?"

I nodded.

"Well, after the shock treatments she became even more psychic, except this time she saw things like people who were going to die or get hurt. But I didn't know this because she kept it all to herself. I read about it in her diary, after, after she…she took her own life."

"Oh, no," I cried. "I'm so, so sorry, Patty." I put my arm around her shoulder and held her as she wept.

Moments lapsed.

"It happened in the river," she continued sorrowfully. "She just couldn't take it anymore. All she saw was death. A few days before her accident, she wrote that she saw a car hit Billy, the little boy next door. She tried to warn his mother without actually telling her that she saw it happen. You know, she would find ways of telling people to be careful, especially when it came to kids. So she'd mostly just create some story that would get people to pay attention to what could possibly happen rather than the thing itself. People already thought she was crazy anyway, and if she suggested anything about knowing what would actually happen to a loved one in the immediate future, since, well, she had been put in this hospital after all, she'd make up stories just so she could convince them and make them prevent whatever was going to happen."

Patty sighed, "She made up one for this lady about there being an epidemic of sickness at the school and suggested to her that she leave her son at home that day. But the mother didn't pay her any mind, and the kid got hit running home after school, right at the pedestrian crosswalk.

"What happened to him?" I asked, quietly.

"He was killed."

"How awful!"

"She felt terrible. She wrote that it was a triple tragedy."

"Why a triple tragedy?"

"Well," Patty went on, "first, she saw a tragic death before it happened. Secondly, the death happened just as she predicted. And third, no matter what she did, no one believed her. So, finally she came to see this 'gift' was not a blessing at all, but a curse.

"Oh, my gosh. This has all been so terrible. Your poor mother."

Patty nodded sadly. "The hardest part in her diary for me to read was that she had visions about her own death. Can you imagine? These visions came to her almost every day. She saw herself jumping into the river and drowning."

"But surely," I interjected, "she would have listened to herself. Right?"

"Yes, she did until...."

"Until what?"

"Until she had another vision," Patty said. "Another vision about what happened to her after she died."

"After?"

"She described her vision of after-death with only a few words. Peace, home, love."

"So, you think that's why...."

"Yes. But she also explained in her little red book that she felt she was unable to use her gift *here*."

"What does that mean?"

Patty looked me in the eye, "Well, I think she meant being alive. She was very frustrated about what she was supposed to do with this gift she called a 'curse.' She prayed to God that He would give her a sign so she would know what to do. She said that when she had these talks with God, it was the only time she felt at peace."

"Did she get a sign?"

"She never said. She wrote that she knew her place was in Heaven though, and that only in Heaven would she be able to be close to me and Daddy."

"I don't think I understand."

"This is what she wrote." Patty gazed at the blue sky above and quoted in a soft voice, "'Maybe, on earth my voice is too loud for people to hear. Maybe, in Heaven, I'll whisper in their ear and they will finally listen.'"

"Your poor mother," I repeated. "How terrible, to be so tortured. God, I can't begin to imagine what that's like, to actually see tragedies from the future and have no power to change their outcome."

Patty gazed forward and said, "There is beauty despite the pain, a beauty that lives beyond death."

I marveled at her statement. It seemed almost poetic, as if she'd heard this from somewhere else. I didn't really understand what this was all about, and yet felt that what she said was right. Her words and her mother's words touched my heart.

"After my mother died," she continued, "I couldn't talk, and I wouldn't eat. I just wanted to be with my mother. My dad didn't know what to do. Our doctor finally suggested I come here, but he didn't want me to after what happened with mother."

"Why did he put you here then?" I asked, with a tinge of anger.

"Well, they convinced him that what happened with mother was unavoidable, not his fault or anyone else's. Only after the doctors convinced him they could help me, did he finally consent to my being here...but on one condition."

"What?"

"That if I didn't get better, he would take me out of here." I stared at Patty and said, "You seem better; you're able to talk and express yourself well. Why are you still here?"

"Actually, I didn't talk and wouldn't eat for several months. And then they suggested shock treatments."

"Oh, no! But you didn't have any, did you?" My heart hurt for her.

"No, thank goodness. Actually, in the beginning, my dad didn't want me to, and he refused to sign the consent forms. It was only after I started to talk again that he made a confession."

"What was that?"

"He told me that the same day he was going to sign the forms, I began talking again."

"Wow! You're really lucky, Patty."

"He called it a miracle and cried a bit, but I still couldn't tell him why I really started to talk again."

"Why? What happened?"

"So, one night, when I was all alone in my room, I heard a voice. I looked in the corner of my room and I saw my mother." Patty stopped talking and looked up, reliving that moment, and then said in a soulful voice, "She looked *so* beautiful, *so* glorious. There was a glowing light all around her and I knew she was with God."

I could feel my eyes widening, "Did…did you talk to her? I mean…how did you know this was real...not just some illusion or dream?"

"That is difficult to explain. All I can say is that what I understood at that moment felt true. She didn't talk—like you and I are talking right now—but I knew what she was telling me."

I interrupted, "Didn't you think you were going crazy?"

Patty calmly looked at me and answered, "No. She spoke to me with thought-words and told me that I needed to stay on earth. She told me I had to eat again, to get better, and that I had an important job God wanted me to do."

I looked at Patty with amazement, but she laughed. "Really, Sarah, after all we've shared together, I do believe you doubt me."

"No, but I honestly don't know what to think," I replied truthfully. "What was it like, I mean, to see your mother floating in your room and you carrying on a conversation with her?"

Patty drank in my question as if for the first time. "I suppose it reminds me of being in church. Just like you don't doubt the love of God, I didn't doubt the love of my mother and her presence there...it was very real. I just knew."

"I think I know what this may mean now. I have felt God's presence before in my life, though I don't think I've actually seen Him himself beyond some images in paintings." I thought for a moment of Michelangelo's vision of God on the ceiling of the Sistine Chapel. I had seen the copy in an art book.

"But you see, my mother has been with me ever since. You should have seen me eat the day after her first visit. The doctors were so impressed that, after a week, they saw no need for treatment. My dad was thrilled and wanted to take me home right away, but they felt that I could easily have a relapse. Since Dad had to go away on a business trip, he agreed to keep me here but planned to come get me as soon as things settled."

"Weren't you sad though to be left here ?" I asked.

"Yes, at first. But then my mom said that I was supposed to stay for a while, and I would know why when the time came." She looked at me and said, "Then I met you and I knew."

"What did you know?"

"I knew that I was supposed to help you."

"How could you know that?"

"After my mother told me I needed to stay, I kept on the lookout for what I was supposed to do here. I tried being nice and helping different people, like Bobby, and others, but not until I met you did, I know," she explained.

"Oh, I get it. I was a real basket case!" I joked.

"Well, I did help, didn't I? "she laughed.

"Yes, you did, Patty." I put my hand on hers. "Honestly Patty, I know I couldn't have survived this long here without you. I'm very grateful, but I'm certain that you are a great help to others, not just me."

She looked at me appraisingly, "I suppose, but you are a very strong person, Sarah. My mom said you are destined for great things."

"Yeah...right," I shrugged dismissively, turning my head toward the window. I knew my life had been ruined. Sitting here, I knew nothing would ever be all right again.

"She wanted me to give you a message." Patty said, in an altered voice.

"What?" My head turned back to her; my jaw dropped. "She had something to say to me? Really?"

Patty spoke with such firm determination it reminded me of a priest professing words from a pulpit, "Yes, Sarah. She told me that you need to believe in your heart—no matter what happens—and that, eventually, everything will be okay."

"Your mother sure talks a lot for being—gone." When those words left my mouth, I realized they were in very bad taste, unkind. "Oh gee, Patty...I'm sorry."

"No, Sarah. That was funny in a hospital sort of way. Don't worry, I get the joke." She stopped and expressed heart-felt concern, "I know this is very difficult to believe. I understand."

She put her hand on mine. "I understand."

I wanted to cry. "At least you have someone."

"Well, sort of. You never know, maybe she'll even talk to you if you're good," she joked.

"What do you mean good?" I made an evil face and we both laughed.

"All you have to do is believe, open up your heart and listen to the whispers in the wind."

"But what if I don't hear anything?" I asked, having become used to disappointment.

"My mother has assured me that no matter what happens, the power of your faith will lead you to happiness."

I felt a sudden anxiety rising up within me that met in equal measure to suspicion, "Sounds to me like I'm not going to survive it here. Is that what you're trying to tell me?"

"No. That's not it," she argued. She sat composed and silent. The corners of her mouth began to curl up. She looked straight at me and said confidently, "You'll know, just like me, if my mother talks to you, you'll feel good, and, and you'll just know, that's all."

"Oh," I said, somewhat mollified. "Do you see her often?" I asked.

"I know she's with me, though I don't feel her presence as much as I did at first. But she came to me last night."

"Isn't that scary?" I asked.

"Not at all, Patty responded. "It seems perfectly natural, believe it or not."

Patty had a way about her. I didn't doubt what she told me. We sat quietly for some time. I noticed Samuel again, doing his performance without a care in the world. I let out a little laugh as I thought of something.

"What is it?" she asked.

"I was just wondering if your mother is one of Samuel's invisible friends," I ventured.

"Huh. I never even thought of that. You could be right; maybe she is."

We both watched him. His arms moved slowly, and his head tilted up as if in some sort of communication with the spirits.

"I wonder," I piped up, "if the spirits are entertained with him?"

"What would they do without him?" Patty laughed.

As the moments passed slowly by, despite the good feeling of Patty's presence, a growing sense of worry began to enter in and finally set heavily inside of me. The air became too thick to breathe.

Patty noticed the shift in my appearance. "What is it?" she probed with concern.

I began to cry. She reached over and held me in her arms, stroking my head. "Don't worry, Sarah, don't worry."

I began to sob, "I—don't—want you to—leave."

"I want to take you with me. I'll try, Sarah, I will try my hardest," she assured me.

After a quiet moment, she said softly, "I know it has been very difficult for you, but you are not alone. Even if I do leave, and even if you can't join me, you will not be alone. I know my mother will look out for you. I know she will."

Patty looked up into the air, deep in thought. She looked so sad.

"I know," I spoke up, "you don't want to stay here. Nobody wants to be here, and you miss your father. I know. I want you to go. Maybe I'll be all right even though I don't feel like it. Maybe your mother is right. Who knows?"

Patty sat quietly next to me, holding my hand, fiddling with my fingers.

"If it were up to me, my father and I, and any decent person for that matter, would not have you stay in a place like this—nobody should. Everyone needs love. I love you Sarah. You're like a sister to me, and I am going to try and do my best to convince my dad to have you stay with us," she said.

I peered at her and smiled bleakly. Something inside told me that was not going to happen. I didn't know what my fate was, but what Patty told me about her mother gave me a whisper of hope. I didn't know why. I just felt it deep inside.

However, other thoughts were crept into the depths of me too. Fears popped up in my head that I didn't like; her dead mother talking to her is completely crazy. I must be crazy for wanting to believe her. Every time thoughts like that entered my head, they left me feeling hopeless. I knew I couldn't take my mind in that direction. I continued to try pushing the dark thoughts away and strove even harder to keep what Patty said in perspective and to stay positive.

After our talk, we didn't do much. We walked around some, holding hands. Later, when Patty took me to my room after dinner, we hugged, and she sat with me on my bed.

"Sarah," Patty began, "I wanted to tell you about my mother only because she was the only one that convinced me to get better and that I had another purpose in my life. I knew in my heart that she was not dead, but she was in Heaven, helping me and helping you too. You have to believe me."

"I'll try, Patty. I'll try."

"It's important to realize that if I chose to remain in sorrow, I wouldn't be going home soon.

That's why I want you to remember your uncle, so he will know that you remember him, and he'll want you to come home too."

Patty stood up to leave. "Don't leave me Patty. I'm afraid. Don't you see? I'm afraid to remember." I blurt out, sobbing.

Patty sat back down and held me in her arms until my broken breath returned to normal. She gave me a kiss on the forehead.

"Thank you for staying," I said. "Thank you for being my friend."

"Please, Sarah, don't worry. My mother…" she paused and gave me a tender look, "My mother said that you will be fine, and that you are destined for great things."

"Do you believe her? Do you really think so?"

"No. I don't just *think* so, I *KNOW*, that's all. I simply know," she said, with something close to irritation in her voice.

"All right Patty," I acquiesced, feeling thwarted, somehow. "I'll try. I really will try to remember more."

After Patty left, I couldn't help but cry. I felt weak and unwilling to face any memories. The nights were always the hardest. The darkness and the haunting sounds played tricks with my mind.

As I lay in bed, I listened for 'whispers' from Patty's mother. I heard nothing. And I was grateful, if truth be told, not to hear the promptings of a ghost.

When I thought about our conversation earlier and how Patty didn't have to have shock treatments, it dawned on me: consent forms! Her father had to sign a consent form before she could get shock treatment! Someone had to have signed mine. Was it my Grandmother or my uncle?

My mind began racing with fear. I wondered what I would do when Patty left. What will happen to me? What will happen when he returns? Will I have more shock treatments?

My thoughts spun to Samuel. Why did I even think he's normal? Why did he talk to me and no one else? Maybe he could tell that I'm crazy like him.

My thoughts started flip-flopping in my head like a fish off a hook. Maybe I'm not crazy and everyone else is but I really don't know. I could be crazy. So could Patty and her mother, but I don't think I'm crazy, and then again, what if I am?

My head swayed back and forth with the thoughts that rolled repeatedly in my mind. I grabbed the sides of my head trying to stop it from thrashing about and trying to stop the scrambled thoughts from echoing, but they wouldn't stop. Why can't I stop thinking like this? Why am I even here?

"I want to leave. I have to leave right now!" I cried aloud. I jumped out of bed and ran to my door. I turned the knob, but my hand slipped over its surface. It wouldn't move. I ran to the window and shook the bars, but they would not give way, no matter how hard I tried. I can't stay here! Patty, I need you, but you're leaving me. Why are you leaving me? I began to cry and fell to the floor for some length of time, I couldn't tell how long, until finally all of the voices in my head quelled. I felt empty and exhausted.

I got up and went back to bed and sat. I brought my knees up to my chest and just stared through the barred, high-set windows into the moonless night. I wanted to sleep and to forget everything. After a long time, a strange sense came to me, yet it felt familiar. It seemed as though I were no longer alone.

I looked to the side of my bed and I saw Patty's face as if she were sitting next to me. Her words echoed repeatedly in my mind, "You have to remember, Sarah! You have to remember so you can go home...go home. Yes, that's what I want. I want to go home. I want to see Grandmother. I have to remember so I can finally go home, just as Patty said. I lay there dazed, staring into the darkness, waiting for my memories to return.

I lay there for over an hour watching the twinkling of stars. As I began to fall asleep, visions from my past seeped in slowly until finally, I had no choice but to remember.

In Flight with the Devil

September 1938

I get out of bed to open my window and realize that my head is still spinning. I walk slowly and find my way to my window seat. Right when I open it, the evening breeze refreshes my face so much I want to rest my head on the cushion and fall asleep right there. I gaze at the round moon then look back at my cozy bed and decide otherwise. Now, if I can only get back to bed without falling down!

My foot manages to find the book I left on the floor. I stumble and luckily plop right into bed. Scooting under the covers, I think back on the evening. We went to the resort for dinner and dancing, but Uncle Joseph let me drink too much! I don't think I like it. My head hurts. We had fun dancing though, and Grandmother seemed to enjoy herself, talking to everyone.

Even though my mind is busy with the evening festivities, I am too sleepy and still dizzy. While I'm deciding that tomorrow would be a much better day to reminisce, I begin to drift into my dreams.

My heavy eyelids struggle to open. I notice that it is still dark, not morning. Suddenly, I feel movement beside me, a body lying next to me under the covers and I gasp!

Uncle Joseph begins stroking my head and says, "Don't be frightened, my little one

"What are you doing?"

"I've been meaning to tell you something very important and we made a pact that we could always share our thoughts no matter what, haven't we?"

For some reason I can't move. I don't know what to say or do. The smell of liquor, not just wine, on his breath is strong.

"It's about you Sarah. I've noticed ever since our first meeting that you have grown into quite a young lady. Your breasts are blooming beautifully." He lowers his large hand to cover one of my breasts.

Fear freezes my mind and body.

"Don't be embarrassed Sarah, you are now a young woman and I felt it my duty, as your uncle, and the only man in your life, to explain to you what that means," he whispers softly. "Most young girls today do not know what it means to be a young woman until much later in life, but I think times are changing. Consider me your private tutor."

I'm finally able to blurt out, "Uncle Joseph, what are you doing, what do you want?" I pick up his hand and push it away. He grabs my hand and holds it down firmly. I can't move it.

"I am admiring you." He lifts up my pajama top and the full moon casts fragile light upon my young breasts. "My, they are beautiful. Look at them Sarah, they're round and full. You certainly should be very proud of your womanly figure." He bends his head down and begins kissing my breasts.

I push his head away with my other hand, but he raises his body and grabs my other wrist. "Owe!" I screech.

He thrusts my wrists up above my head then holds them both with one hand. I can't escape his firm grasp. My body freezes. When he turns, his eyes stare right into me. His eyes appear empty. I am terrified and shut my eyes.

While squeezing my wrists even harder he commands, speaking under his breath, "Don't say another word, Sarah, you will regret it."

I look at him determined to stop him, but I've never seen those eyes before, and I know he means every word. I feel it. Tears well, filling my eyes. I'm so very afraid and scream inside. He has to stop! However, something tells me that no matter what I do, it has already happened.

"I am going to show you the magic of your body," he commands. Then, his voice becomes soft, as if what he is doing is usual and expected. "This will not be at all difficult; it will be easy for you. I will instruct you slowly, but I am sure you won't make any mistakes, so don't be frightened or worried."

"No," I whisper, meekly.

"Sarah. Don't speak. No matter what."

I look at him and again his eyes spell certain terror. I close my eyes and pretend this is nothing but a bad dream. I think that if I pretend hard enough, he'll just disappear but he doesn't.

"Becoming a woman will be very natural for you, unlike most young girls. You are special and beautiful. I really mean that. You have a magnificent body and you should be proud of it." His hands stroke my belly and move slowly over my breasts.

"The first thing you will feel is strange or awkward. This is how you are supposed to feel, Sarah, it's perfectly normal. After I show you the magic of your body, you will explode with ecstasy and delight."

The more he talks, the more I can't think. I start crying and just want to hide.

"Your body has magic spots." Uncle Joseph puts his hand again on my breast. He squeezes and twists my nipple with his fingers. "Do you feel the magic?" he asks.

I want to scream, 'don't touch me', but terror holds my words captive.

"Yes, feel the excitement, Sarah, feel the pleasure," he says. "Now I'm going to show you the best part," he says and reaches down and slips off my panties.

"No," I whisper. "No, Uncle Joseph. Why are you doing this?" I'm embarrassed. Tears run down my cheeks.

"Shush," he says softly.

He acts as though I am not relevant, and he is acting out a secret pleasure where I have absolutely no say. He pays no attention to me, yet says it is for me. I don't understand. Is this supposed to be happening?

"There is a place," he explains as his hand stretches down and presses my crotch, "Do you feel it?"

"Uncle Joseph, no," I say softly, "that's not nice. Why are you doing this?"

I can smell him breathing on my face. He whispers in my ear, "Do as I say, or else."

I try to move away, and he squeezes my wrists harder, feeling like they would soon break. My body relinquishes to his control and falls still.

Uncle Joseph smiles and says, "I can see you feel the warmth of love rising in your body. You are a woman, a beautiful, beautiful woman. Now say 'Joseph,'" he demands, "I want you to say 'Joseph.'"

I say nothing.

His command repeats.

Faintly, the word slips over my tongue but hold no meaning, "Joseph."

"Say it again, 'Joseph', 'Joseph'," he repeats quietly, in his deep, determined voice.

I repeat the empty words, "Joseph, Joseph... Joseph."

The thought of what is happening swims around my head with no place to hide, no place to go. I'm so utterly embarrassed. I want to close my eyes and forget it's happening, but Joseph takes my hand and places it on his crotch. I start to spin inwards, running away faster than his words can catch me, my face burning in shame.

Joseph's whispers become even more excited, "You did right, Sarah. Now it's time to make me feel the same pleasure you felt." I pull away my hand. "No, Sarah. You can't stop. That wouldn't be fair at all," he orders sternly. "You need to learn what makes a man feel good too."

He grabs my hand and guides it to the hardness between his thighs, up and down with a squeeze, repeatedly. "A man enjoys something around him that's wet. Joseph yanks my hair and then pushes my mouth down over his hard appendage.

I try to forget as it happens, as if it isn't real. I want to cry and scream for him to stop, but it's too late. I begin to choke and feel like throwing up.

"Don't stop, Sarah!" Joseph pulls my hair up and pushes down my head. "Don't stop Sarah."

Joseph's body quivers until he moans repeatedly.

I'm choking and coughing. I can't breathe, but Joseph holds my head in place. I feel dizzy, like I'm going to faint when he lets go of my hair.

I lay frozen in shame and guilt.

Joseph's tone quickly and completely changes. "Go and wash your face and bring back a towel to wipe up this mess. Do it fast and don't make a sound!"

I put on my robe and do as he says. When I return, he grabs the towel, wipes himself, drops the towel on the floor, and then stares at me. I cannot move.

The light of the full moon reflects an insidious glow in his eyes, like that of a wild beast. He commands firmly, without hesitation, "You are not to say anything to anyone about what you did tonight." He places his hands on my shoulders gripping them tightly. "This is between us and no one else." The corners of his mouth turn up slyly and he says, "It's our little secret."

Joseph puts his robe back on that he draped over the chair next to my bed and stands close to my shivering body. I feel heat radiating from his body and smell his sweat and semen. My stomach begins to turn. Again, he places his strong hands firmly on my shoulders and squeezes hard. "Now you are a woman."

All I can think is, "No, I don't want to be a woman. I don't want to be a woman."

He turns away, beginning to leave and then stops. His voice elevates in severity as he speaks, "Don't forget, Sarah, you're not to talk about what you did tonight, not to anyone! Do you understand?"

I stare at him without emotion. Even though I am nauseous and feel I am about to faint, I remain stoic for I know if I make any sound at all, he will hurt me.

"Now get to bed," he demands and shoves me down onto my covers. "You'll get over it and want more. I know all about it. If you think about telling anyone how you touched yourself and how you touched me, remember that I can hurt you Sarah. I can hurt you really bad."

I don't want to hear anything he is saying. I try my best to block his words, but they echo over and again in my head, "You touched yourself, you touched me." My face burns in shame.

As he starts to leave, he stops once again and turns. He walks with slow determination, puts his face in mine and says, "I have no fear about causing pain as I have no fear about bringing pleasure. Remember that. I have no fear, Sarah. Let's hope you never have to experience the pain I can cause you—or Mother."

That same icy evil look emerges again in Uncle Joseph's once handsome eyes. My shaking will not stop, and I try to hold myself still. He can't see me shake.

He says, seeming to delight in the thought of causing pain, "Dear Grandmother. What would she think if she found out what you did, Sarah? I wonder. Maybe we should tell her." his face grimaces before slowly transforming back into a shrewd smile. He blows me a kiss, and as he walks out, he says, "Sweet dreams, little angel. Sweet dreams."

I look down at my bed. I can't sleep here, not after.... I try to figure out what I can do and decide that I will just have to change my sheets, but all I want to do is cry.

Suddenly, my door opens. Uncle Joseph whispers, "Remember Sarah, I'll be watching your every move." He turns and walks out, leaving my door ajar.

My eyes fixate on the door for fifteen minutes. I hear nothing but the chime of our grandfather clock echoing up the stairs. I pray softly, "Dear God, please don't let him come back." Finally, the silence gives me courage to wash up and secure a cover-up.

I know that I can't take a bath—It would make too much noise—so I clean myself up from the filth and sweat he slathered all over my body. I apply an abundance of my sweet jasmine powder with my big white puff and I slip on a clean nightgown and robe. Then, I take off my sheets, clean up my bed and get new sheets. I sob quietly while I make my bed as neat as I can, tucking in the sheets and blanket tight. I take the filthy sheets, robe and soiled nightgown, place them in my hamper, and then splash what's left of the glass of warm milk over the pile.

Once in bed, I curl myself up into a tight ball and begin shivering uncontrollably. I try to convince myself that I was just dreaming, but my body tells me otherwise. I feel like a beast, an evil serpent in the Garden of Eden, slithered in and ravaged me. How am I ever going to face anyone or go to church again?

I try to convince myself that what had just happened in the shadows and moonlight of my room was nothing but a nightmare, a horrible, horrible nightmare. I want Nan to be here, to hold me and keep me safe, but my burning shame freezes my soul. I try to imagine if he were to come back what I would do, but I can't think of anything.

Uncle Joseph, now unleashed, knows no limits. He visits my room almost every night ensuring pain entwined with sensual pleasure. As the nights turn into months, each moment of every day I live and breathe an overwhelming desire to shut out personal contact with anyone, to harbor my soul within invisible walls built by me. I made a pact that I had to protect me, my soul no matter what he does. I made a pact that someday Uncle Joseph will have to pay for what he has done to me. I learn to put up a front, a shadow of what I used to be. Real happiness that I took for granted is now beyond my reach. Each day takes me further and further from the reality of that first night. As the sense of who I really am drifts away; I am lost within the bounds of no desire, in flight with the devil.

Outside of Time

B arbara carefully took the last page of the chapter, turned it face down on top of the stack. Images of him raping Sarah persisted in plaguing her imagination. She got up and went to the sink to get a glass of water. It was night and she looked out the window at the dark sky and cityscape with its flickering lights.

A terrible thought emerged. I wonder if other little girls are being molested at this moment. She felt chills of disgust as she looked out on so many households and apartments that surrounded her. How terrible, she thought. How awful.

As she stared out the window an image appeared. It was like a ghost, a face of a young girl with blond hair just on the other side of the glass. Her eyes pleaded for help, but Barbara knew that she could do nothing. She touched her cheek and wiped the tears. I hope that I can help you Sarah. I don't know how, but I hope.

Barbara looked towards her bedroom and knew she wouldn't be able to sleep right away. She went over to her tall bookcase, hoping to find some fluff to read to calm her. I should read something light and not long, she told herself.

Her eyes perused the books until she found one that she loved since she was a child. *The Golden Treasury of Poetry*. She opened to a page and read aloud, "In the beginning, they tell us, there was nothing but joy in the world. Everything was bright and new. Earth and sky had just been made. Man was a child, living in a Paradise which was a cross between a great garden and a divine playground. Every morning was a fresh surprise."[iii] She smiled, gently, imbued by the innocence of childhood and took her book with its well-read tattered pages to her room and read until she fell fast asleep.

I awoke anxious about the day. Barbara was due to arrive an hour early and I wondered if the chapter about my uncle's night visit was too graphic. What will she think? I simply felt embarrassed about the subject matter, but it was Sarah's story.

In the middle of organizing my papers for our talk, Tara startled me with a series of short barks when the ring of our doorbell sounded. "Is it nine already?" I looked over at Tara.

She barked incessantly. "Be quiet!" I shouted. "It's only Barbara." When I opened the door, her barks turned into whines with an attitude as if she were saying, "I want to see her, I want to see her too!" Her body twisted and curled with excitement. Wagging her tail wasn't enough. She had to wag her whole body.

Barbara came in and bent straight down to Tara. "Let me say 'Hi' to her first or she'll never forgive me," she smiled up at me meaningfully, while giving Tara's silky ear a gentle tug.

I laughed. "You know her so well already."

She looked up with her nose in the air, "What did you bake today? It smells divine."

"Banana bread," I said, pleased. "I'll slice some for us."

"Looks lovely," Barbara said, when I gave her the slice. We nibbled on the bread and sipped hot coffee. All the while, Tara begged for more crumbs.

Barbara looked at me. "Are you alright?" I sighed. "Just really anxious about you reading such a horrific scene."

"What can I say?" she began. "No wonder Sarah was so disturbed." She paused then quickly added, "Or should I say 'you'."

"No. Don't say 'you'. It is not this life. However, the memories felt as though they were."

Barbara gave me such a warm smile, that I almost teared up. "Do you think it is too graphic?" I asked. "I mean, did I say too much, explain too much?"

"That's a tough question," she looked at me thoughtfully. "Honestly, I felt embarrassed while reading it, but isn't that what you want? Don't you want other people to feel what you felt?"

"Not really," I said.

"You know what I mean," she responded.

"I know. It is difficult. Just think, even a lifetime later it is still embarrassing, painfully so," I confessed.

"I can understand. Some things will forever be embarrassing to us," Barbara replied, then wondered a moment if she should tell Kerry about not being able to sleep. She half-laughed and said, "To be honest, I had to get out one of my favorite childhood books to help me get to sleep last night!"

"Oh no! I'm so sorry."

"No, don't be," she assured me. "It's real and I think it has to be said."

"Thank you, Barbara. That means a lot to me." I began fumbling through my papers and in the process told her, "I have to tell you that I was reading over what I had written about other molestations by Uncle Joseph, but I don't think it is necessary to include them in my book."

"What would be the point?" she asked, and added, "Had you chosen to do so, the story would undoubtedly collapse into the prurient, and then you'd have a very sleazy graphic novel with the type of writing that would only appeal to the truly sick and depraved."

"True. The whole point is to make certain that others understand how devastating incest is, that it doesn't haunt a person just in their present lifetime, it can plague them in the following life—maybe even many lives after that."

"But first," she stated matter-of-factly, "someone would have to believe in future lives, and that is asking a lot of most people."

"I'm not asking people to believe just because I say it. I want them to consider the possibility and reach deep into their soul and seek the truth. The fact still remains that they cannot know for certain until they pass on or recall a past life with certainty as I have."

"Well," Barbara emphasized, "even if a person believes only in one life, incest and molestation is extremely devastating."

"Yes. I've also considered the effects of someone reading my book who has been abused or sexually molested as a young boy or girl. What if they carry an urge to do the same harm to others, an overwhelming urge that takes them out of the concept that there is a future? My hope is that my book will offer reason to change these impulses."

"What do you mean by the idea of no future?" she asked.

"The incest or molestation experience is so devastating and difficult to accept, that I believe it is placed outside of time into memory's darkest shadows. If someone were inclined to abuse others because of their own abuse, they too would be doing it outside of time with no concept of the future and the effects on themselves and others from their harmful acts."

Barbara interrupted, "You're losing me."

"Okay. What don't you get?"

"What do you mean by being outside of time?"

"Well, most people have a conscious time-line of their life. Their sense of what happened yesterday is closer in time than it is to what happened ten years before or when they were children. This is the sense of time. Where do repressed experiences go, experiences that are too awful to put on the memory time-line? I believe they are placed outside of time into their own mental Pandora's Box. Therefore, these subconscious experiences are always present though out of sight."

"Hmm, an interesting concept. How did you come up with that?" Barbara asked.

"It is an idea born out of my own investigation into the effects of incest and molestation on Sarah. Once I faced and detailed the experience in words, I was bringing it out of the darkness, into the light and placing those memories back to a moment in time."

"Are you saying that because someone can't face or be present when they are being molested or if they are molesting someone, it doesn't exist on a timeline?"

"In a way, I am for the most part. I can't say for everyone though. But, imagine if you were Sarah," I began when she interrupted.

"Oh, I certainly did last night."

I made a pouting face. "Sorry. What I mean is, what she experienced was so awful, that the mind, to protect her, has a failsafe. Those moments become repressed. The horror becomes repressed and it's not able to process."

"I think I'm getting it!" she said. "Makes me think of a safe room in a house where bad guys can't come in!"

"Good image."

"You're saying it's a natural human response like experiencing a battle in war or any awful situation that is difficult to face."

"Yes. I think it's because our true nature is love eternal. What Sarah experienced is the antithesis of love." I paused a moment then added, "I was able to put her moments of horror back to its timeline. I took it out of Pandora's Box and back into the realm of love where there is hope for healing."

"It's interesting that you say that."

"Why?"

"Remember when you read to me the definition of Pandora's Box."

"Yes," I answered.

"When Pandora opens the box and all the troubles in the world were released, only hope remained under the lid. That indicates that one has to look under the lid to find hope and you looked under the lid."

"Wow! That's amazing. I never thought of that!"

Barbara sat up tall and proud, put her hand to her waist and slightly bowed. "You are welcome," she said then laughed.

"When I think about Sarah, in a sense, I have a relationship with her. A duty. I believe she wants me to tell her story, not for her, but for all the voices bound by shame and fear and cannot speak and whose words have no page to write on.

"I believe that words are what set us free, whether written or spoken. Words are created from the truth of that which is, which is why I love etymologies. Words can carry the enormous weight of a terrifying moment or the lightness of love."

"Now who needs to bow," she said and giggled.

I bowed my head down. "Thank you." I want you to know that I'm not saying it's easy to face and resolve. But I am saying it's possible." I looked off and began gathering my ideas as Barbara waited. "As an artist I have an ability to observe. This ability requires an emotional detachment, like what does it *look like* versus what do I *think* it looks like." Barbara nodded. "This ability is probably why I can look at a problem, like a leaky trap under the sink and figure out what to do other than freak out!"

I laughed. "I'll call a plumber, thank you. That reminds me. Debbie called one day, and my husband answered the phone. She asked where I was, and he said under the sink!"

"That's funny. But not everyone has that skill of keen observation," she added.

"Precisely. However, just like finding a plumber, one can find a skilled professional to help sort out these 'outside of time' experiences and bring them to the forefront where it can be processed. The thing is, it's not about accepting what someone says your experience is. It's about finding the right words, or whatever, for yourself to fully grasp the experience. Once that is done and a person feels that release, there is no reason to 'beat it to death.'"

"I don't know," she answered. "I think it would be so overwhelming to try to overcome the damage from such evil or to suddenly accept responsibility for the harmful acts if one is the actual abuser."

I thought for a moment about her comment, then shared my own belief, "That may seem impossible and feel impossible, but dreams can come true. I believe in God. I have complete faith from my own experience. There is such a thing as real healing from the tragedies of life. But healing requires a willingness on our part. That's the key."

"There is hope then, "she said.

"You know, Barbara," I began, "Sarah's story along with my story of facing it, is an attestation of that being possible. By sharing with others my struggle to discover the truth in my Pandora's Box, they will see how I found truth and it may provide hope for them to find their own way."

"It seems to me," Barbara said, with a purposeful look, "that you have thought quite a long time about this. Did your awareness of this happen back in 1977, when you first had the sessions?"

"Oh, no," I stated. "I did become aware of some incidents of incest from that life. The first actually happened in a small guest room, just off the kitchen, which I don't include in my story."

"Why not?" she asked.

"After I wrote about many of the terrible events from this Hell of a previous life, I decided one day to read, from beginning to end, the whole debacle of what I'd written down. I sat at home on my couch and began reading from page one." I shook my head, stating, "It didn't take long to realize how depressing it actually all was. I thought to myself, 'Why would anyone want to read one bad thing right after another? There have to be moments of light in all the darkness.' Which is why I decided to look for pleasant moments from Sarah's life and include them in my book."

"I understand."

"Although viewing and documenting the horrors were difficult, transcribing it onto paper helped me tremendously. I was able to see more of that life and bring back parts of my soul that had been claimed by the tragedy."

"If it's any consolation, you seem happy and, how can I say, confident in a courageous sort of way. Like no matter what, you will survive!" I smiled.

"Thank you for that. But what you're seeing in me now took lot of time viewing and documenting these awful events within my past life. Prior to this laborious process of writing every major event in Sara's life, I started recognizing that I was unusually clairvoyant and then later realized that I've actually had these unusual abilities my entire life."

"You've mentioned that before."

"Yes. I slowly discovered my intuitive side helped me with the process tremendously."

"How?"

My head was down a bit thinking, and I glanced up at her with raised eyebrows. "I soon discovered that as I helped Sarah, my clairvoyant gifts allowed me to begin helping others, along with myself. The more people I helped, the more clairvoyant I seemed to become."

"That's fascinating. Tell me more!"

I looked at the clock. "I hate to stop now, but I have to go and pick up some art supplies for my class this afternoon."

"I understand."

"Would you like to go with me? It's not far."

"Sure. Do they have journals there?"

"Yes, they do."

"Great. So we'll continue the story tomorrow?"

"Yes." Then I teased, "I'll also share with you my experience I had about St. Francis when I was on a pilgrimage tour to France and Italy in 1989."

"Can't wait!" she said, and then quickly added. "What about Sarah and her story?"

I thought about the next few chapters that were in a folder on the table and wondered what to say.

"What are you so serious about?" She asked.

I smiled. "I guess you can read my thoughts now."

"No, but I can feel that something is bothering you."

I grabbed the folder tightly in my hand and said, "These next two chapters that I'd like you to read are a bit unsettling."

Barbara quickly asked, "Are they as dark and disturbing as the 'Flight with the Devil' one?"

"Not as much."

"Then I'm good," she stated with confidence and quickly took them out of my hand.

"Boy, you are amazing."

"Well, *I'm reading about* incidents and experiences that you recalled. Yes, it is disturbing but I can't imagine how that made *you* feel."

I thought for a moment and said, "Honestly, the more I wrote, edited, reread and edited again it became less difficult. Also, it seemed that every time I faced the darkness of that life the opposite would occur, and I began having miracles."

"I can't wait for the reprieve!"

We both laughed.

I looked at her and smiled. "Barbara, I just want to say how much I appreciate you coming over, listening to my stories and reading my book."

She put her hand on my knee and said, "I'm happy we met. And I have to add I don't think it was a coincidence after all!"

I smiled and said, "I agree."

Epilogue

F̲ollow both Sarah's and my crusade in *Hands of God*, the next book in series, where witnessing and writing about Sarah's experiences bring unexpected gifts and profound miracles.

Not only do these blessings grant me fortitude and courage to forge ahead as I continue transporting myself into Sarah's life, they bolster my hope to heal both of our severed hearts.

Sarah's journey to learn the truth about her past continues with Patty and Samuel's help where she discovers an inner strength, a strength she will need.

As my gift of seeing beyond the normal realm of sight bourgeons, I discover a calling to help others and when I do, amazing miracles, small and large begin to manifest. One of these miracles along with its story is the inspiration for the title of book two, *Hands of God,* in the *Divine Miracles* series.

To view the painting from my vision please visit my website.[1]

---

[1] https://kerryvandyke.com/fine-art/

Artwork

Cover Design

DESTINY

In the midst of writing my story about my past life a vision came to me along with these words;

I hold my sword high into the air and charge against evils encased in darkness.

To represent my vision entitled *Destiny*, with the words included, I wanted the canvas to be large and constructed the stretcher bar frame to be 7.5' x 4'. Once prepared, I painted a frame which borders the vision and then painted sections of the words centered on each side. I cropped off the frame for the front book cover but the original painting, along with the back-cover art (for print books), can be viewed on my website[2].

The vision is a dark silhouette of young woman standing atop a mountain. Behind her are the Himalayas. A thin white line along with aura colors outline her body. Centered in her heart is a subtle blue radiating out that represents the hope of healing. In her left palm she balances a silver sphere.

---

[2] https://kerryvandyke.com/fine-art/

With her sword held high she pierces the darkness through two clouds shaped from my two hands gently closed over with the thumbs almost touching. In the heavens above the clouds, are stars, the crescent moon and one shooting star.

This painting which hangs on my wall is a joyful reminder that I am not alone and continues to bless me with the determination and courage needed to face the most unimaginable evil.

Back Cover

WINDOW IN TIME

The painting on the back cover is called *Window in Time*, which was my initial title for my book. The vision for the painting came to me when I pondered looking through a window in time into my previous life.

The painting has four sides and each of the opposite sides are not parallel. The longest lengths are 8' vertical and 2'-4" horizontal. The top of the image is filled with the darkness of the heavens and about halfway down the sky gradually becomes blue. In the night sky are a multitude of stars, a full moon and the Milky Way on the right with several shooting stars. In the blue sky near the bottom is the sun with rays emanating out.

Sketches

In this book are a few sketches of buildings, people and landscapes that became vivid in my mind when I entered my previous life. Drawing became another way for me to feel and understand what happened. Each time I drew, the energy and emotion of the experience transferred onto the page through my line work.

Acknowledgment

I want to thank my three editors. Michelene Landseadel, 'Miki one', who was my first editor and continues to help with editing and insightful suggestions.

Also, Betty Starr-Joyal (1934-2015) my second editor and Miki Vohryzek-Bolden, 'Miki two', who also graciously helped with editing.

About the Author

Kerry Van Dyke was born and raised in Sacramento, a city by two rivers between the Sierra Nevada Mountains and San Francisco. Both of her parents were loving and creative. Her father was an architect, artisan, hobbyist and loved the outdoors. Her mother was a gifted pianist and avid reader.

As a young child Kerry discovered that she could draw and paint just about anything. and as a teenager she excelled in writing fiction and loved journaling. When she was in her late thirties, she discovered her spiritual eyes and began helping others with this gift. Because she is reflecting someone's truths, she often jokes that she may enjoy the readings more than the client because she gets to see and know more than she ever could have imagined.

Kerry has always been a truth seeker, whether with art, writing or giving intuitive readings. As an artist and wanting to share her art and artistic skills, she opened her own business in 1986 aptly named "Kerry's Art," and continues to produce art and teach small and private art classes. As a writer she loves philosophy and to express with words as she would a painting.

Kerry resides in Sacramento, CA and has two daughters, Carissa and Lara, who currently live in Chicago, IL.

If you want to know when Kerry's next book will be released, please visit her website, www.kerryvandyke.com.

NOTES

[i] "Pandora's Box." *Merriam-Webster.com. 2020.* Online https://www.merriam-webster.com (28 June 2020)

[ii] By Eleanor Farjeon (1922). The hymn originally appeared in the second edition of Songs of Praise (1931)

[iii] Golden Press, Inc. 1959, Rockefeller Center, New York, N. Y., p. 9

Made in the USA
Columbia, SC
23 January 2021